Reason, Virtue and
Psychotherapy

Reason, Virtue and Psychotherapy

Antonia Macaro

John Wiley & Sons, Ltd

Copyright © 2006   Whurr Publishers Ltd (a subsidiary of John Wiley & Sons Ltd)

The Atrium, Southern Gate, Chichester, West Sussex PO19 8SQ, England

Telephone (+44) 1243 779777

Email (for orders and customer service enquiries): cs-books@wiley.co.uk
Visit our Home Page on www.wiley.com

Other Wiley Editorial Offices

John Wiley & Sons Inc., 111 River Street, Hoboken, NJ 07030, USA

Jossey-Bass, 989 Market Street, San Francisco, CA 94103-1741, USA

Wiley-VCH Verlag GmbH, Boschstr. 12, D-69469 Weinheim, Germany

John Wiley & Sons Australia Ltd, 42 McDougall Street, Milton, Queensland 4064, Australia

John Wiley & Sons (Asia) Pte Ltd, 2 Clementi Loop #02-01, Jin Xing Distripark, Singapore 129809

John Wiley & Sons Canada Ltd, 22 Worcester Road, Etobicoke, Ontario, Canada M9W 1L1

Wiley also publishes its books in a variety of electronic formats. Some content that appears in print may not be available in electronic books.

Library of Congress Cataloging-in-Publication Data

Macaro, Antonia.
    Reason and virtue : a framework for psychotherapy / Antonia Macaro.
      p.   cm.
    Includes bibliographical references and index.
    ISBN-13: 978-0-470-01944-3 (pbk. : alk. paper)
    ISBN-10: 0-470-01944-1 (pbk. : alk. paper)
    1. Philosophical counseling.   2. Aristotle. Nicomachean ethics.   3. Conduct of life.   4. Reason.   5. Virtue.   I. Title.
    BJ1595.5.M33 2006
    171'.3 – dc22

                         2005036215

British Library Cataloguing in Publication Data

A catalogue record for this book is available from the British Library

ISBN-13 978-0-470-01944-3 (pbk)
ISBN-10 0-470-01944-1 (pbk)

Typeset in Times and Univers by SNP Best-set Typesetter Ltd., Hong Kong
Printed and bound in Great Britain by TJ International Ltd, Padstow, Cornwall
This book is printed on acid-free paper responsibly manufactured from sustainable forestry in which at least two trees are planted for each one used for paper production.

Our account will be adequate if its clarity is in line with the subject-matter, because the same degree of precision is not to be sought in all discussions, any more than in works of craftsmanship. . . . So we should be content . . . to demonstrate the truth sketchily and in outline, and, because we are making generalizations on the basis of generalizations, to draw conclusions along the same lines. Indeed, the details of our claims, then should be looked at in the same way, since it is a mark of an educated person to look in each area for only that degree of accuracy that the nature of the subject permits. Accepting from a mathematician claims that are mere probabilities seems rather like demanding logical proofs from a rhetorician.

(Aristotle, *Nicomachean Ethics*, Book I, Chapter 3)[1]

---

[1]All text citations of Aristotle are taken from the Crisp edition in the References.

Contents

About the Author

Antonia Macaro is an existential psychotherapist and philosophical counsellor. She has many years' clinical experience in the field of addictive behaviours. For a number of years she has been exploring the practical uses of philosophy, particularly Aristotelian virtue ethics. She is a supervisor and visiting lecturer at the New School of Psychotherapy and Counselling, London.

Acknowledgements

I would like to thank all the friends and colleagues who read all or part of the first or second version of this book, and in particular Gerald Rochelle for his extensive and useful feedback. Also thanks to David Arnaud and Tim LeBon for our joint work on practical philosophy and decision making over a number of years – I am sure that even just the idea of writing this must to some extent have been inspired by those conversations. Thanks to Windy Dryden for encouraging me to pursue the idea. Finally, thanks to Colin Whurr and everybody at John Wiley who has in any way been involved with this project.

Introduction: A Therapy for Sisyphus

That life is suffering has been known for millennia. In Buddhism this fact is considered so important as to constitute the foundation of its whole system of thought and discipline. Unlike other animals we are able to reflect on our efforts and their results, and in the light of our considerable limitations we may come to see ourselves as puny and irrelevant creatures. Death seems to cast a shadow on all our achievements and endeavours.

It can indeed seem very puzzling: we are born, live a life in which suffering is inevitable and die, without any obvious explanation for this lamentable state of affairs. So we ask ourselves what life is all about, whether it has any purpose, whether it fits into some mysterious grand scheme that could somehow provide answers and make us feel more important. Without those answers, our daily efforts and strivings can seem utterly insignificant, and the hustle and bustle of a working day appear no different from the mindless activity of ants toiling up an anthill.

Camus (1975) sought to capture this sense of pointlessness through the image of Sisyphus. In the Greek myth Sisyphus was condemned by the gods to spend his life pushing a boulder up a hill without ever succeeding: the boulder would perpetually roll down and Sisyphus had no choice but to push it up again and again, in full knowledge that his efforts would never produce the desired results. Camus used this as a powerful metaphor for the human condition.

Human beings are blessed – or cursed – with the ability to see themselves 'from the outside'. While on the one hand we take ourselves and our projects very seriously indeed, on the other we are able to reflect on this and see that in the greater scheme of things we do not matter that much. It does not matter whether we fulfil our potential, get married, have a promotion or become enlightened. In a sense, it would not really matter if we were not here at all. The recognition of this discrepancy between a perspective in which we take ourselves so seriously and one in which we recognise our status as just another animal living on a planet that will be destroyed in a few million years has been seen as the source of our feeling that life is absurd (Nagel, 2000). Many people have found such thoughts depressing.

There have been and still are answers that can give some of us relief. According to these our life is given meaning and purpose by virtue of being part of something bigger, such as the plans of a god, or gods. This connection is questionable, as Nagel (2000, p. 180) vividly explains:

> If we learned that we were being raised to provide food for other creatures fond of human flesh, who planned to turn us into cutlets before we got too stringy – even we learned that the human race had been developed by animal breeders precisely for this purpose – that would still not give our life meaning, for two reasons. First, we would still be in the dark as to the significance of the lives of those other beings; second, although we might acknowledge that this culinary role would make our lives meaningful to them, it is not clear how it would make them meaningful to us.

Belief in soothing religious answers has anyway become more problematic because of the likely clash between such answers and what science tells us about the world.

It could be said that the growth of counselling and psychotherapy in our times is directly related to a confusion about how to make the best use of our time on earth, given the loss of old certainties, the lack of sound uncontroversial guidance and the seemingly bleak picture painted by science. It has been pointed out that those who seek help nowadays are more likely to suffer from a sense of meaninglessness, emptiness, depression and lack of values than from traditional neuroses (Guignon, 1999), and that the people who are flocking to counsellors and psychotherapists to examine their lives would in the past have been catered for by priests and rabbis (compare for example, Frankl, 1959).

Some forms of psychotherapy arose specifically in response to this need. Viktor Frankl (1959), a concentration camp survivor and the founding father of logotherapy, wrote of our situation in terms of an 'existential vacuum': an inner emptiness, a void, that arises as a result of the fact that we are guided neither by our instincts like other animals, nor by the traditions that seemed so solid before. What we need to do, in his view, is to give up our search for an abstract meaning *of* life and instead create our own unique meaning *in* life, looking for the particular values that can give us fulfilment and a sense of purpose. Logotherapy was designed to help people to do just this: become creators of their own values and responsible for their own meaning.

Similarly, existential psychotherapy aims to address the fundamental features of existence that give rise to our puzzlement and anxiety: death, freedom, isolation, meaninglessness (Yalom, 1980). Whilst the label functions more as an umbrella term for a cluster of related practices than as a single defined approach (Cooper, 2003), there are certain shared characteristics. These include working with the clients' lived experience and helping them to accept the responsibility of authoring their lives when no absolutes are available apart from existential 'givens'.

While other forms of therapy may be based on models and explanatory systems that depart rather more from the clients' existential realities, it could be argued that the existential vacuum left by the loss of traditional values and world-views lies behind the extraordinary success of the 'talking cures' in general.

In an article entitled 'The Age of Therapy', reporting the results of a recent research project commissioned by the British Association for Counselling and Psychotherapy, the *Counselling and Psychotherapy Journal* (Nov. 2004) states that 'Britain is today a "therapy nation" in the making' (p. 46). The project found that 72 per cent of adults 'believe that people could be happier if they talked to a therapist about their problems'. The authors see these results as reflecting a change in society as a whole as well as in our values. We are wealthier and less constrained by traditional standards, so we have more opportunities to make choices about who we are and how we want to live. This gives rise to a host of new stresses and anxieties, about which we might want to consult a therapist.

The conclusions that Camus drew from Sisyphus's predicament were on the whole uplifting: it is possible to find meaning even in eternally pushing a boulder up a hill. But for a latter-day Sisyphus, it would appear, the struggle to find that meaning will often involve some kind of therapy. Therapy seems here to stay.

DIANA AND THE SOCIOLOGIST

The public outpouring of emotion after the death of Princess Diana in 1997 has been seen as a deeply symbolic event, marking a profound shift in the mood of the nation from buttoned-up and stiff-upper-lip to emotionally aware and relaxed about displays of feeling. Many saw this as a good thing. Others did not. One of the latter was Professor Frank Furedi, a sociologist, who considered the phenomenon part and parcel of an unhealthy 'therapy culture' that is precipitating us towards dependency and unreason.

Furedi (2003) describes what he calls 'therapy culture' as an ethos in which people are encouraged to exchange autonomy and self-reliance for a dubious cult of the emotions. While in the past many life difficulties would have been seen as a normal part of the human condition that we simply had to learn to take in our stride, it is now assumed that we do not have the resources to do this: 'Through pathologising negative emotional responses to the pressures of life, contemporary culture unwittingly encourages people to feel traumatised and depressed by experiences hitherto regarded as routine' (p. 6). Hence the perceived need for professional help to sustain our fragile and vulnerable selves. While this gives the illusion of support, in reality it enfeebles people and creates a climate of dependency.

According to Furedi, our therapy culture is self-absorbed and narcissistic to the point where the language of self-fulfilment and self-expression overshadows moral and political concerns: 'Instead of right and wrong, there are only different ways of feeling about the world' (p. 73). He connects this with the decline of tradition, religion and politics. Therapy has filled a void caused by 'the erosion of a system of meaning through which people make sense of their lives' (p. 86). This system of meaning created connections with accepted ways of doing things and a wider sense of purpose. Its decline has caused fragmentation, anxiety and a narrow focus on the individual self. Previously, religion offered a way of making sense of inner experience that could be shared with others. That role has been taken over by the much more introverted context of therapy.

Taylor (1991) makes related but broader points about the climate of modern American society. One of the trends he criticises is a facile relativism according to which everybody has his or her own values, about which it is impossible to argue. This is linked with what he calls 'the individualism of self-fulfilment' (p. 14): a world-view prescribing that everybody should choose his or her own lifestyle on the basis of self-determined values that are beyond challenge or discussion. Instead of following others in attacking this narrow culture of self-fulfilment as selfish and self-indulgent, however, Taylor recognises that it is based on the reasonable moral ideal – however degraded – of being true to oneself.

It is easy to overstate the case. The effort to become more autonomous and the search for a more meaningful life seem perfectly good things, as do awareness of our emotions and the ability to manage them at times. But the accusations that the contemporary therapy culture is plagued by emotionalism and subjectivism have a point. While this is by no means equally true of all the therapies in the marketplace, there is undoubtedly a generalised therapy ethos that to some degree devalues reason and objectivity, favouring instead intuition, inner truth and the expression of emotion.

This has numerous downsides: our emotions can be inappropriate and do not always point us in a helpful direction; trusting our 'intuition' can amount to little more than acting on unexamined prejudice, and it can go disastrously wrong; what 'feels right' is not necessarily so; our 'inner truth' needs to be reconciled with everybody else's; and it is not the case that in the sphere of values and ideals 'anything goes' – it is not just a matter of choosing, it is a matter of choosing well.

But these are not the consequence of a therapeutic ethos *per se*. They are rather the result of a *particular* therapeutic ethos. It is not a recent phenomenon to regard the emotions as potentially problematic and in need of management. The philosophies that developed in ancient Greece held that belief. The recipes they offered to deal with the problem, however, were in many respects different from our own, since they embedded human flourishing in human nature and gave reason a central place in a good human life. They therefore provide an apt counterbalance to the emotionalism and subjectivism of our times.

'HOW SHOULD I LIVE?'

When we think about ethics or morality, we are likely to think in terms of duties and obligations, or rules and principles that should guide our actions. This was indeed the focus of the two main traditions that came to dominate modern ethics: deontology (derived from the philosophy of Immanuel Kant) and utilitarianism (based on the thought of Jeremy Bentham and John Stuart Mill). According to the former, we should act out of respect for the moral law; for the latter, our actions should be guided by the fundamental moral principle of producing the greatest good for the greatest number. While these two approaches are usually seen as antagonistic to each other, they do share the view that human beings are bound by universal duties and that moral reasoning consists in the application of principles (Statman, 1997).

But there is a third major ethical perspective to consider, one that started to develop a few decades ago out of dissatisfaction with the prevailing theories. It was argued that our legalistic conception of ethics was essentially the remnant of a religious framework, and that in a secular context it made little sense to continue to focus on thinly disguised divine commands (Anscombe, 1958). Anscombe advocated a return to an Aristotelian view of ethics, based on human flourishing and the virtues rather than on any concept of law. This initiated a new wave of ethical thinking that took inspiration from ancient philosophy and that came to be known as 'virtue ethics'.

Ancient ethics begins with the question 'How should I live?' This was the starting point for a great deal of philosophising. But the question itself is not only a philosopher's question: it is a deeply felt one that many reflective people will ask themselves at some point, wondering whether their life is what it should be or whether it needs to be improved in some way. The answers to it cannot be ready made, and for reflective people they are likely to be informed by philosophy. According to Annas (1993), 'Ancient ethics gets its grip on the individual at this point of reflection: am I satisfied with my life as a whole, with the way it has developed and promises to continue?' (p. 28). It is this emphasis on whole lives and on issues of character and choice that seems to resonate with our own lived experience in a way that modern ethical theories do not.

The first philosopher to write systematically on ethics as a distinct topic was Aristotle. His main text, the *Nicomachean Ethics*, is widely regarded as a set of lecture notes rather than a book intended for publication. The question of how to live was also the focus of the later Hellenistic schools, such as the Stoics and Epicureans. These, however, proposed answers that were more extreme and divergent from common sense. It was Aristotle who put the concept of 'virtue'[2] firmly on the agenda for the good life, so it is not surprising that he figures prominently in the virtue ethics literature. But what do we mean by 'virtue'? A good working definition to begin with might be that '[a] virtue is a character trait that human beings, given their physical and psychological nature, need to flourish (or to do and fare well)' (cited in Statman, 1996, p. 31).

---

[2]*Virtue* is the traditional translation of the Greek word *aretê*. This is also sometimes translated as *excellence*, but in the sphere of ethics it refers primarily to matters of character.

The vocabulary of human flourishing and the virtues can enrich therapeutic work with clients who are grappling with issues such as finding meaning in life, making difficult choices or reflecting on what kind of person they would like to be. If clients are concerned with some aspect of how to live a good life, Aristotle is a good guide to the territory. This book does not advocate an alternative to therapy or a new method in therapy.³ Rather, my aim is to present a broadly neo-Aristotelian virtue framework that can be used to guide and structure explorations of the good life when client material so requires. Adopting this perspective as a tool can help therapists to direct the clients' attention to areas that warrant investigation, ask relevant questions, attend to crucial distinctions and assist them in examining ideals, making choices and dealing with life dilemmas. Needless to say, counsellors and therapists may also use these ideas to inform their own search for the good life.

While this is in some ways a common-sense perspective, it is also at odds with many accepted beliefs and practices in the field of counselling and psychotherapy. The emphasis on reason, for instance, may seem out of place if we believe that the role of therapy is to discover unconscious motives, get people 'in touch with their feelings' or awaken their intuition. There are greater similarities with approaches that focus on the exploration of values and/or beliefs, such as existential and cognitive psychotherapies.

The perspective I present is neo-Aristotelian in the sense that the overall structure of the book is based on what I believe to be the most relevant topics in Aristotle's *Nicomachean Ethics*. I also endorse many of Aristotle's views about the topics covered. But the book is emphatically not about exegesis. While I hope to have remained faithful to the spirit of Aristotle, my account is not limited to highlighting features of his theories that could be useful in working with people's life dilemmas, but also draws on ideas from other thinkers and models. I have ignored the anachronisms that we inevitably find in Aristotle's work (such as his views on women and slaves) since I do not believe these to be relevant to the aspects of his philosophy discussed here.

Choice of terminology can be a thorny issue. For reasons that will become apparent (see Chapter 1), I have not used 'happiness' to translate the Greek word *eudaimonia* (the good life, human flourishing). I

---

³The fairly new discipline of philosophical counselling, which draws on philosophical ideas and methods to help people with aspects of their lives, is sometimes put forward as a clear alternative to psychotherapy.

have on the other hand adopted the term 'virtue', despite its slightly quaint and outdated connotations, since it is well established in the philosophical debate, and through Positive Psychology it is also becoming accepted in the psychology arena. I do not believe in a definitive boundary between counselling and psychotherapy, and therefore I use the terms interchangeably.

Aristotle stressed that ethics should make a difference to how we live and therefore guide our reflections on the good life, the decisions that we make, our willingness to follow those decisions and the character traits that we aim to develop. Unfortunately his writings on the subject do not always make for enjoyable reading. It has been said that Aristotle 'has a dry conciseness that makes one imagine one is perusing a table of contents rather than a book; it tastes for all the world like chopped hay' (cited in Quennell, 1988, p. 168). Hence the many tomes devoted to interpreting the intricacies of his thought are, however, unlikely to be of great practical assistance in how to live well. This is a shame, because Aristotle has a lot to offer us in our search for the good life. My hope is that in this book I have been able to give a flavour of Aristotle that does not taste like chopped hay, raise questions for reflection and above all offer some perspectives that can be put to good use in fostering more fulfilled and worthwhile lives.

STRUCTURE

In Chapter One I consider a number of possible 'ingredients' of the good life and present an Aristotelian 'recipe' that gives value to many aspects of human life but primacy to practical wisdom and the virtues of character. I discuss the foundations of such a recipe. I point out that this is by no means a rigidly prescriptive view, since it needs to be adapted to particular individuals' lives. I pay some attention to how this could be used in working with clients, by helping them to clarify and think through what is important and valuable in life and how their ideals connect with the reality of their lives. This chapter provides the framework for the rest of the book, and its excursions into somewhat more theoretical grounds are necessary for that purpose.

In Chapter Two I expand on practical wisdom. Following Aristotle, I associate this with the ability to make wise decisions. This involves being able to apply our knowledge and ideals to particular situations. I discuss the skills this requires, such as self-knowledge, critical thinking and generally being able to identify good reasons for action. I discuss the pitfalls of 'intuition'. I consider how we can help clients to identify the right thing to do in a particular situation by, among other things, shedding light on real and supposed value and disentangling reasons from excuses.

Chapter Three is devoted to the virtues of character. I present an Aristotelian view of these, which involves acting and feeling according to reason. This is characterised in terms of achieving the 'mean' between the opposite flaws of excess and deficiency. While the areas in which virtue may be called for are too many to fit into a neat list, I highlight some areas in which the exercise of virtue is likely to be required in any human life. I describe how the virtues are developed by training and look at how we can help clients to assess which traits and qualities to encourage in themselves and which to curb.

In Chapter Four I discuss two competing attitudes towards the emotions, one that glorifies and one that vilifies them. I consider the question of what an emotion is before returning to an Aristotelian position about the appropriateness of emotions. How can we decide whether an emotion is appropriate and what should we do if it is not? Managing our emotions can be an important step towards developing the virtues, and I present a number of ancient and modern methods that have been found useful in doing this.

In Chapter Five I look at the important area of self-control. This is a step down from the virtues, but is the next best thing if we have engrained habits and attitudes to fight against. In particular, we need to learn to train ourselves to act appropriately in cases where there is a discrepancy between judgement and motivation. Again, this is a step towards the development of the virtues. I consider the parallels between lack of self-control (or 'weakness of will') and addictive behaviours, as well as some methods that could be used to counter either of these.

Finally, in Chapter Six I look briefly at some of the objections that have been made to reason-based models and conclude that, while our notion of 'reason' needs to be cut down to size, it does not need to be thrown out with the bath water.

1

'How Should I Live?'

IN SEARCH OF THE GOOD LIFE

There is a question in life that at some point is likely to acquire urgency for many reflective people – including therapists and their clients. This question is: 'How should I live?' It can also be expressed as: 'What is worth pursuing in life? How can I live a worthwhile life? How can I avoid wasting my time in this world?' This distinctly philosophical set of concerns often ends up being explored in a psychotherapist's consulting room.

Aristotle, among other philosophers, thought that there was an answer to this question. Not just a range of answers, varying indefinitely across individuals and/or cultures, but an answer common to all human beings by virtue of their being human. He was among the first philosophers to treat the good life as a defined topic of enquiry, and although he wrote a long time ago much of what he had to say is still relevant to our own search for a worthwhile life. Aristotle assumed that there was a universal aim in life and that this was *eudaimonia* – the good life, human flourishing. But, as he himself acknowledged, to say that people want to flourish and have a good life does not take us very far in finding out what that means in practice. His method for ascertaining this was to begin with common views about the good life and put them through critical scrutiny. I will follow him and consider pleasure and happiness, wealth, success and relationships – all common topics in counselling and psychotherapy – before turning to such central issues as reason and the virtues.

HAPPINESS

Happiness is big business nowadays. It is commonly assumed that our aim in life is to be happy. Gurus, workshops, self-help books and therapeutic techniques jostle in the marketplace to sell us happiness. Scores of people seek some kind of therapy because they want to be happy. But what is happiness?

Our terminology is confused and confusing. Our ordinary concept of happiness is entangled with that of pleasure, and both are vague. The word 'pleasure', for instance, can suggest a physical sensation, such as what we may associate with a massage, but can also refer to the more diffuse sense of enjoyment we could get from walking in the woods in the autumn, learning the tango, looking at a Vermeer, listening to the *adagio* from Schubert's String Quintet or talking with a friend. 'Enjoyment' covers a similar area but is broader, with weaker physical connotations. 'Happiness' is even more unspecific, and while we could talk of being happy when enjoying any of those things, the term is often used to refer to a generalised sense of well-being and contentment.

But the main characteristic of this happiness–pleasure cluster is that it refers to a subjective feeling or mood. The view that this feeling or mood is the most important ingredient of the good life is a common one and is known as *hedonism*, from the Greek word for 'pleasure'. From the dawn of philosophy, some form of hedonism has often been held to be the truth about the good life.

The idea that happiness as subjective experience could be the most valuable thing in life is challenged by a widely quoted thought-experiment known as 'the experience machine':

> Imagine a machine that could give you any experience (or sequence of experiences) you might desire. When connected to this experience machine, you can have the experience of writing a great poem or bringing about world peace or loving someone and being loved in return. You can experience the felt pleasure of these things, how they feel 'from the inside.' You can program your experiences for tomorrow, or this week, or this year, or even for the rest of your life . . . . Would you choose to do this for the rest of your life? If not, why not?
>
> (Nozick, 1989, pp. 104–5)

We would not remember entering the programme once we were in it, and we might even program in uncertainty in order to provide variety and prevent boredom. Could this be a good life, the best possible life? Most people do not think so. This shows that on reflection most people do not consider pleasant experiences the most important thing in life. What matters more than how experiences *feel* is that they are *real*: we do not want to just *feel* that we have climbed Everest or written a great symphony; we want to have actually done so. Achieving these things may not always be *pleasant*, but may nevertheless be worthwhile and give meaning to our lives.

Aristotle's discussion of pleasure as a potential candidate for the role of the main ingredient of the good life hinges on the distinction between being pleasant and being worthwhile. His views about pleasure of the physical sort seem damning at first: people whose main interest lies in bodily pleasures live lives that are 'fit only for cattle' (*Nicomachean Ethics* [hereafter cited as *NE*], Book I, Ch. 5). We might therefore be excused for thinking that Aristotle is advocating a life of self-denial. But this could not be further from the truth.

Aristotle's defence of pleasure takes mainly two forms:

1. *There are different types of pleasure, and they are good or bad in different degrees.* The word 'pleasure' can be applied to a range of experiences, only some of which are to do with satisfying bodily appetites, while others may instead result from being absorbed in study or other worthwhile activities. This is a distinction that has tended to recur in the history of philosophy and reappears, for instance, in J. S. Mill's distinction between higher and lower pleasures.
2. *Even purely bodily pleasures are good in moderation.* We are embodied creatures, and Aristotle recognises that a certain number of 'goods of the body' are important for a good life: 'for everyone enjoys fine food and wine and sexual intercourse in some way, but not everyone in the way he ought' (*NE*, Book VII, Ch. 14). Bodily pleasures can be harmful and distract us from more worthwhile pursuits, but it is only *excessive* indulgence that is damaging, not the pleasures themselves. Too little appreciation of these can also hinder our pursuit of the good life.

Bodily pleasures are therefore acceptable and even good within reason, but we can also redefine our understanding of 'pleasure' to mean the kind of enjoyment that is an intrinsic part of being involved in any worthwhile activity. Here it is not the attainment or otherwise of pleasure that determines whether an activity is worthwhile; on the contrary, pleasure results from the value of the activity. Although both kinds of pleasure have a place in the good life, the latter is the better and more lasting. According to Aristotle, it just *is* pleasant to, say, study philosophy.

We can probably think of several counterexamples to this: activities that we value but do not particularly enjoy at the time, such as studying for an exam, helping a friend through a depression, running a marathon for charity. We may be glad to *have done* these things, but that is different from enjoying them *at the time*. Aristotle occasionally admits that enjoyable or pleasant experiences and worthwhile ones do not always coincide. Of course there is no reason why things should not be pleasant *and* worthwhile, but the point here is that when the two do not coincide it is by no means a foregone conclusion that enjoyment should trump other kinds of value.

The Greek word *eudaimonia* – the good life, human flourishing – was traditionally and still is mostly translated as 'happiness'. But it is widely acknowledged that this translation is misleading, since our notion of happiness as a momentary and subjective feeling is miles away from the Greek ideal of *eudaimonia* as applying to a whole life and based on what that life was actually like rather than what it *felt* like.

The thinness of our concept of happiness as compared to the richness of *eudaimonia* has been recognised by a number of authors. Grayling (2003, pp. 27–8), for instance, writes that by *eudaimonia* Aristotle meant 'an active kind of well-being and well-doing. . . . The English word "happiness" . . . embodies a very pallid conception in comparison: one could make everybody happy by putting suitable medications in the water supply, but that would scarcely convey what Aristotle had in mind.'

Similarly, Marar (2003, p. 8) condemns our concept of happiness in vivid terms: 'The very idea seems untextured, toothless, "happy clappy". The concept belongs in some virginal fairyland, bleached of nuances and subtlety. The terrain of real life, criss-crossed by pain and beauty and smells and tears and dignity and ideas and eroticism, simply cannot have its contours reflected by such a shapeless notion.' He also points out that the ancient concern about how we should live has nowadays been replaced by a narrower focus on what we really want, in what he calls 'the subjective turn': instead of a comprehensive question about a whole life, we have adopted a much more limited question about self-fulfilment and self-expression.

Feelings of happiness are part of what we want in life, but other things may be both more important and unrelated to the felt quality of the experience we are having. As Nozick (1989, p. 106) points out, 'there is more to life than being happy'. That enjoyment is not always the most important value is corroborated by stories about individuals who choose to devote themselves to something worthwhile and absorbing – research, say, or human rights – that entails making sacrifices and foregoing the pleasant experiences that they could otherwise have had. After what was by all accounts a tormented existence, the philosopher Wittgenstein's last words were: 'Tell them I had a wonderful life.'

If this is the case, to which should we give priority? Should we fill our life with pleasant episodes or sacrifice immediate enjoyment for the sake of worthwhile achievement? Ideally a good life should contain a balance of both: a life that has had many worthy achievements but hardly any enjoyment seems a bit grim, and conversely a life that has seen many enjoyable times but has not been guided by some worthwhile goal seems vacuous and superficial.

Another conclusion that has been drawn is that happiness should be a 'side-effect' of living a good life rather than something that we seek for its own sake. According to Nozick (1989, p. 113), happiness 'rides piggyback on other things that are positively evaluated correctly'. He also writes that, 'We want experiences, fitting ones, of profound connection with others, of deep understanding of natural phenomena, of love, of being profoundly moved by music or tragedy, or doing something new and innovative, experiences very different from the bounce and rosiness of the happy moments. What we want, in short, is a life and a self that happiness is a fitting response to' (p. 117).

WEALTH

Wealth is another ubiquitous aim for human beings. And yet we have no trouble thinking of examples of people who are very rich and very unhappy. It is a cliché that money cannot buy happiness (although perhaps it can make unhappiness less uncomfortable). What is the proper place of wealth in the good life? Since most people adopt this as a goal, it needs to be at least considered as a candidate.

Aristotle has no time for this, and dismisses this claim briskly by saying (*NE*, Book I, Ch. 5) that, important though money is, it is only a means to an end: 'wealth is clearly not the good we are seeking, since it is merely useful, for getting something else.' It follows from this that a life devoted exclusively to the accumulation of money would not, for Aristotle, qualify as good. This seems right. It is almost always what money can give us that we want, rather than the money itself. What it can give us is leisure time, opportunities, comfort. What we (wrongly) think it can give us is self-esteem and freedom from worry.

There are a number of problems with making the value of our lives depend excessively on the acquisition of material goods:

1. Spending our life in the pursuit of material goods (bigger cars, houses, designer clothes) is likely to prevent us from devoting our time and energy to more important and worthwhile things. Thoreau (1983, p. 73) expressed a similar sentiment when he wrote that 'the cost of a thing is the amount of what I will call life which is required to be exchanged for it, immediately or in the long run'.
2. These goods are flimsy, in the sense that their retention is not always up to us, and we could never absolutely insure against their loss; therefore it seems unwise to rely on them for our well-being.
3. It is a well-known fact about human beings that as soon as a desire is satisfied another will take its place, so that pursuing the good life in this way could end up as a wild goose chase.

At the other extreme are those who renounce their wealth. The philosopher Wittgenstein, for instance, chose to give away his family fortune. An even more extreme choice is to abandon a life of luxury for a life of renunciation. According to the legend, Prince Siddhartha Gautama, later to be known as the Buddha, walked away from his father's palace in the depth of the night – leaving behind wife and son, renouncing all worldly goods – and took himself off to live a life of contemplation and self-denial in the forest. He spent a few years as a wandering ascetic, meditating and fasting. He did not allow himself to have sufficient food, clothing, shelter – all things that we normally consider fundamental to a good life.

Is it possible to have a good life if we are cold and hungry? Perhaps it is not impossible, but it would certainly be a challenge for most of us. Aristotle (*NE*, Book X, Ch. 8) thought that a certain number of basic goods[1] was necessary: 'because the happy person is human, he will also need external prosperity; for human nature is not self-sufficient for contemplation, but the body must be healthy and provided with food and other care'.

Even the Buddha arrived at the conclusion that extreme renunciation was not the right way to enlightenment, and that a more moderate path was a better way. However, Aristotle warns us that this is not the ingredient that makes a life flourishing:

we should not think that someone who is going to be happy will need many substantial things, just because one cannot be blessed without external goods. For neither self-sufficiency nor action depends on excess,

---

[1]Basic goods include, but are not confined to, material goods: reasonable health, for instance, is an important prerequisite for a good life.

and we can do noble actions without ruling over land and sea, because
we can act in accordance with virtue even from modest resources.

(*NE*, Book X, Ch. 8)

Although a moderate quantity of material goods is a prerequisite for a
good life, and great misfortune will prevent someone from having a
truly blessed life, even in very unfortunate circumstances what really
determines our quality of life is not the circumstances themselves but
what we make of them:

> For the truly good and wise person, we believe, bears all the fortunes of
> life with dignity and always does the noblest thing in the circumstances,
> as a good general does the most strategically appropriate thing with the
> army at his disposal, and a shoemaker makes the noblest shoe out of the
> leather he is given, and so on with other practitioners of skills.
>
> (*NE*, Book I, Ch. 10)

SUCCESS

Other things that many people want are fame and recognition, so we
need to consider the possibility that it might be these that make a life
good. Aristotle is wary of this, since they are too dependent on the
whims of fortune:

> Honour, however, seems too shallow to be an object of our inquiry, since
> honour appears to depend more on those who honour than on the person
> honoured, whereas we surmise the good to be something of one's own
> that cannot easily be taken away.
>
> (*NE*, Book I, Ch. 5)

The relationship between our own excellence in whatever field and our
being so recognised by the outside world is by no means direct. People
get to the top for all sorts of reasons, and being excellent is not necessarily the most important one: an engaging personality might count for
more, or even a Machiavellian one, for that matter. Conversely, people
may fail to get to the top for reasons unrelated to lack of talent: again,
personality characteristics could get in the way, as could simple lack of
opportunity, or being 'in the wrong place at the wrong time'.

It is also possible to *choose* not to climb the dizzy heights of success,
in the awareness that there is always a price to pay, perhaps in sheer
time, or having to make compromises, or having one's privacy invaded.
Despite having the opportunity to be a university professor, the philosopher Spinoza chose to make a living grinding lenses, devoting his

spare time to philosophy. On the other hand, the pages of magazines are full of the exploits of celebrities who are famous only for being famous. Could this be what we mean by the good life?

Furthermore, success itself is not the point: we do not just want to be recognised, we want to be recognised by people we admire and for a good reason:

> Again, they seem to pursue honour in order to convince themselves of their goodness; at least, they seek to be honoured by people with practical wisdom, among those who are familiar with them, and for their virtue. So it is clear that, to these people at least, virtue is superior.
>
> (*NE*, Book I, Ch. 5)

We could say that what is important is our talent, but according to Aristotle that is not quite it either, since great misfortunes or inactivity can prevent someone from having a good life despite their great gifts or talents. Talent has to be actualised in some way.

And what should we make of cases of posthumous recognition? Did Mozart's and Van Gogh's lives fail to be good while they were alive but suddenly became good when their fortune turned, though too late for them to enjoy it? Aristotle thought that this kind of view would be absurd. Yes, the possible future effects of our actions matter, but they should not matter excessively.

Bertrand Russell's (1975, p. 39) assessment in this respect seems right: 'Success can only be one ingredient in happiness, and is too dearly purchased if all the other ingredients have been sacrificed to obtain it.'

RELATIONSHIPS

Aristotle recognises that human beings are inherently social, and that therefore a good life should include human relationships of various sorts. He thought that we would be hard pushed to describe someone who is totally solitary as having a good life: 'No one would choose to live without friends, even if he had all the other goods' (*NE*, Book VIII, Ch. 1). He devoted many pages to this topic.[2] There are three types of relationships, according to Aristotle:

---

[2]The term that Aristotle uses, *philia*, is traditionally translated as 'friendship' but is much broader in meaning, and covers a range of social interactions – from casual ones with the local shopkeepers or friends we meet at the pub, to romantic and family relationships.

(1) the useful (e.g. business associates);
(2) the pleasant (e.g. people who entertain us with funny stories); and
(3) the ones based on mutual admiration.

Of these, the last kind is the most important, since it is the most solid. The first two are

> ... incidental, since the person is loved not in so far as who he is, but in so far as he provides some good or pleasure. Such friendships are thus easily dissolved, when the parties to them do not remain unchanged; for if one party is no longer pleasant or useful, the other stops loving him.
>
> (*NE*, Book VIII, Ch. 3)

A good life may dispense with business associates and jokers, but it may not easily dispense with the mutual disinterested love and care that distinguishes genuine relationships. These are likely to be few, since an essential aspect of this kind of relationship is sharing joys and sorrows, and it is simply not possible to allocate that amount of attention to many people.

To what extent should we stand by people we genuinely care for if they reveal themselves to be morally other than we thought, or if their behaviour takes a turn for the worse? Should we dump them if they suddenly switch political allegiances, or have an affair, or embezzle money from the charity they work for? What if they commit some hideous crime? Aristotle thought that we should give up on them if the crime were truly vicious, but otherwise we should try to help them to see the error of their ways, even though this would be likely to change the nature of the relationship. Genuine relationships entail a certain amount of agreement on important matters.

When it comes to our attitude towards ourselves, we should cultivate the same feelings of friendliness and warmth that we display towards people we care for. This involves being undivided in our feelings and thoughts, wishing ourselves good things, enjoying spending time with ourselves and generally being kind to ourselves.

How can we disagree with all this? Of course we need people who care for us and whom we care for in order to have a good life. Of course all sorts of other things and achievements may seem empty and futile in the absence of important others with whom to share them. But solitude has its place too. In his writings on *flow*, the psychologist

Csikszentmihalyi (1992) says that solitude can be enjoyed so long as we learn how to structure our attention. He writes that it is important for a well-rounded life to be able to do that, since if we regard solitude as something that should be avoided at all costs we will end up resorting to distracting activities of limited worth in order to fill the gaps. Being alone can be enjoyable and fruitful.

In a similar vein, the psychiatrist Anthony Storr (1989) writes that, important though love and friendships are, they are not the only source of happiness, and they should not be burdened with that responsibility. In fact, many people of genius spent very solitary lives. He mentions the following: Descartes, Newton, Locke, Pascal, Spinoza, Kant, Leibniz, Schopenhauer, Nietzsche, Kierkegaard, Wittgenstein. Creative pursuits and impersonal interests, 'whether in writing history, breeding carrier pigeons, speculating in stocks and shares, designing aircraft, playing the piano, or gardening' (p. xii) can make a life happy and valuable even in the absence of satisfactory human relationships.

In his solitary hut by Walden Pond, Thoreau (1983, p. 180) found that at times of loneliness nature was a better companion than any human being:

> In the midst of a gentle rain while these thoughts prevailed, I was suddenly sensible of such sweet and beneficent society in Nature, in the very pattering of the drops, and in every sound and sight around my house, an infinite and unaccountable friendliness all at once like an atmosphere sustaining me, as made the fancied advantages of human neighborhood insignificant.

Personal relationships are important to a good life and therefore deserve a substantial investment of time and energy. But we should also cultivate impersonal interests and develop the capacity to be alone. We must remember too that it is possible for some individuals to choose solitude and isolation for the sake of other pursuits, such as contemplation.

REASON

Aristotle believed that the main ingredient of a human life is reason, since this is the defining characteristic of human beings. We share growth and reproduction with plants and movement and sense-perception with animals, but reason is what distinguishes us from other known forms of life. While all the things discussed so far are part of the good life, reason is key to it. There are different interpretations of Aristotle on this, but it is plausible to read him as saying that a good life should include the best possible use of *all* human capacities, reason being the central one among them.

A mindless life, one that is not in some way ordered by reason, would barely count as a *human* life: if reason is what makes us distinctively human, a fully human life must include it. But a good human life could not fail to include 'at least some of the satisfactions which arise from our inescapably biological nature' (Cottingham, 1998, p. 40). And our capacity to feel deep emotions, to love, to be moved by music, art, nature is also unique, most certainly part of what makes us fully human. We should value and cultivate all aspects of our humanity (senses, emotions, reason) while realising that they need to be ordered by reason.

Aristotle divided reason into *theoretical* (*sophia*) and *practical* (*phronêsis*). Theoretical reason is about contemplating unchangeable truths. Practical reason (or practical *wisdom*) is to do with deliberation and choice in the sphere of things that can be changed. It is hotly debated which of these Aristotle considered most important. An interpretation that seems to make sense is that ideally – if we were more like the gods – we might want to devote our lives to contemplation, but given that we are mere mortals we need other things as well. As human beings, practical wisdom is perhaps the fundamental way in which our rational nature expresses itself.

It would be difficult to deny that some practical wisdom needs to underpin everything we do, whatever our chosen goals: we would be hard pressed to achieve anything at all without an ability to weigh up, assess, choose, plan, implement, monitor. On the other hand, could we really have a good life without some intellectual curiosity, without seeking to learn and understand? Both are ways of applying our unique capacity to reason, and as such essential ingredients of the good life. In addition, practical wisdom is a way to obtain the other things that make for a good life: it is therefore at the same time an end in itself and a means towards other ends.

A modern endorsement of some of these ideas comes from the literature on *flow* (Csikszentmihalyi, 1992, 1997), according to which we function at our best in situations where we have clear goals and immediate feedback, and skills and challenges are appropriately matched. At those times our attention is ordered, we become totally absorbed in our task and we lose track of time. This is the most valuable kind of experience – more important than happiness, which suffers from being both more passive and more vulnerable to external circumstances. When we are in flow, we cannot be happy, because we are focusing on the task at hand rather than on our state of mind. By learning to control and direct our attention we can increase the amount of flow that we experience in our life.

The idea that flow is active and leads to increased complexity in consciousness seems particularly important. Hurka (1993, p. 123) makes a similar point, albeit in a different context: the best life requires being involved in complex and challenging activities that 'stretch our capacities, demanding more rationality than ones that are simple'. While flow theory is clearly a product of modern psychology, it is Aristotelian in the sense that it identifies a way of functioning that universally makes for a better life, and it considers enjoyment to be best generated by worthwhile activities that involve our cognitive abilities. We should not aim for happiness: we would never reach it. Instead, we should aim to do things that stretch us and help us to develop. Happiness may be a by-product of that.

THE VIRTUES OF CHARACTER

Theoretical and practical reason are *intellectual virtues*, and they are a central part of the good life. But they are not enough: in order to flourish as human beings we also need to develop the *virtues of character* that allow us to *feel* and *act* according to reason. This is the other requirement of a fully rational life. Aristotle suggests that in order to live well we should adopt appropriate ideals, learn to identify the appropriate course of action through rational deliberation and train ourselves to feel and act accordingly.

Practical wisdom is about judgement, about deciding how to act in each given situation: choosing goals, assessing them, deciding what is feasible, appropriate, desirable, considering possible consequences, selecting options, implementing, monitoring. Being virtuous, on the other hand, is about training ourselves to develop the qualities and character traits that will enable us to follow the dictates of practical wisdom with ease.

There are spheres of life that we find it difficult to deal with, and being virtuous is about becoming skilled at handling these, getting it right in situations in which it is easiest to get it wrong. But what does 'getting it right' mean? This is how Aristotle puts it:

> For example, fear, confidence, appetite, anger, pity, and in general pleasure and pain can be experienced too much or too little, and in both ways not well. But to have them at the right time, about the right things, towards the right people, for the right end, and in the right way, is the mean and best; and this is the business of virtue. Similarly, there is an excess, a deficiency and a mean in actions.
>
> (*NE*, Book II, Ch. 6)

Getting it right involves 'hitting the mean' in our feelings and actions, in everything we do. Excess and deficiency are opposite ways of getting it wrong. The right thing, which 'hits the mean', is determined by reason in decision-making. In order to develop a good character we need to encourage in ourselves the tendency to *want* to follow reason, and cultivate the attitudes and habits that help us to have appropriate and balanced emotional responses to things and situations. The virtuous person enjoys acting virtuously and 'is fully unified in motivation and deliberation. He does not have to summon up willpower to do what he sees to be the right thing, for he does not have to fight down countering desires' (Hursthouse, 1999, p. 369). This attitude can be developed by training.

The term 'virtue' has recently been rescued from languishing in philosophy books and Victorian manuals, and been adopted as one of the buzz words of the Positive Psychology movement. Seligman (2003), the guru of Positive Psychology, draws a distinction between positive feelings due to 'shortcuts' (passive pleasures) and those arising from the exercise of strengths and virtues. The latter are more enduring and are the ones that produce 'authentic happiness'.

MINDFULNESS

'Theoretical reason' for Aristotle refers not to learning about the world but to the contemplation of unchanging truths. The boundaries he draws around this concept are somewhat different from those that seem natural to us. We may prefer to use this term in relation to learning and acquiring knowledge. But there is a yearning for transcendence that is also fundamental to human experience and that could perhaps be captured by what we could call 'mindfulness', an attitude of attentiveness and sensitivity to the world around us. This seems an important part of the good life.

One way to experience a connection with the mystery of life is through nature. Russell (1975, p. 191) wrote that it is in a 'profound instinctive union with the stream of life that the greatest joy is to be found': we are creatures of the Earth, and a connection with its rhythms gives us true and profound satisfaction. Our life seems to be enhanced by things that give us a sense of belonging and perspective, putting us in touch with the very big or the very small, and through that with the vast natural processes of which we are part. Referring to a similar concept that they call 'transcendence', Peterson and Seligman (2004, p. 39) write that it 'is that which reminds us of how tiny we are but that simultaneously lifts us out of a sense of complete insignificance'.

We can also experience moments of discontinuity and insight through aesthetic appreciation. Referring to Japanese aesthetics, Grayling (2003, p. 2) writes about 'an attitude of appreciation and mindfulness, especially mindfulness of beauty, as central to a life lived well'. This celebrates ordinary things like 'the patterns of grain in wood emerging after many years, the sound of rain dripping from eaves and trees, or washing over the footing of a stone lantern in a garden and refreshing the moss that grows about it'.

The concept of an 'agnostic spirituality' is less contradictory than it may seem (Batchelor, 1998), and mindfulness is its foundation. Nozick (1989) points out that paying attention to our breathing is a way of breaking down the boundaries between us and the external world, making us feel less like a separate entity and more aware of the web of interconnections in which we exist.

There can be a thin dividing line between a mindful attitude and a religious one, but it could be argued that the difference is great. From an agnostic point of view, the value we can find in life is to be found within it, 'exploring and responding, relating and creating' (Nozick, 1989, p. 110); religious perspectives, on the other hand, often place the value of life outside life itself, in some future realm or divine purposes. But does this really work? According to Baggini (2004, p. 19), looking to God and an afterlife to add meaning to our life is a misguided policy, entailing as it does a leap of faith 'that a God we cannot know to exist has a purpose we cannot discern for an afterlife we have no evidence is to come. Further, we would also be trusting that this purpose is one we would be pleased with'.

It could also be said that any belief that fundamentally clashes with reason should, no matter how consoling, be disqualified from being part of the good life. It may indeed be the case that religion makes people happier, as is often reported, but the price of happiness would be too high if it required lowering our standards of reasoning and evidence. According to Grayling (2003, p. 203): '"fulfilment" could never be understood as meaning some thin, vacuous species of "happiness" that could be produced by . . . acceptance of a system of falsehoods and illusions', and is something that can be achieved 'without the aid of belief in supernatural agencies or adherence to an organised religion'.

THE GOOD LIFE: ONE OR MANY?

Aristotle's account of *eudaimonia* involves 'the full range of human life and action, in accordance with the broader excellences of moral virtue and practical wisdom. This view connects eudaimonia with the conception of human nature as composite, that is, as involving the interaction of reason, emotion, perception, and action in an ensouled body' (Nagel, 1980, p. 7).

Since Aristotle, many others have tried their hand at sifting the essential ingredients of the good life. One such list is: knowledge, rational activity, close personal relations, appreciation of beauty, development of personal potential, moral goodness[3] (cited in Guignon, 1999). And another: accomplishment, basics of human existence (autonomy, enough health and material goods, liberty and so on), understanding (both practical rationality and knowledge of oneself and the world), enjoyment (beauty, nature, 'textures of life'), deep personal relations (love and friendship) (Griffin, 1986). For Grayling, the essential ingredients are: 'individual liberty, the pursuit of knowledge, the cultivation of pleasures that do not harm others; the satisfactions of art, personal relationships, and a sense of belonging to the human community' (2003, p. 203).

Taking inspiration from Aristotle we could say that the good life will tend to involve basic goods (sufficient health and material comforts, liberty and autonomy), some enjoyment, achievement and meaningful relationships with people. But the main ingredients are reason, in the shape of practical wisdom as well as learning and understanding, and the virtues of character. What is important to note here is that what really makes for a good life is *activity* involving reason rather than *possession* of some good or other. And we must not forget that

---

[3]This presupposes the split between the moral and the prudential that is common in modern ethics. But, given the focus on the overall question of how to live, this split is redundant in virtue ethics.

this activity may include imagination, appreciation of beauty, creativity, humour.

Many people will feel that this is too prescriptive. An assumption engrained in our outlook on life is that it is a purely individual matter to determine what the good life is. We might feel that everything is up for grabs, that we create our own values single-handedly, and that there are few or no constraints on how we might choose to live. We are the ultimate judges: any choice is as good as any other so long as it pleases us. If we decided that the good life for us consists of eating chips in front of the television, this would not be open to challenge. According to Taylor (1991), this kind of view can be traced back to three eighteenth- and nineteenth-century ideas: (1) that human beings have an intuitive sense of what's right and wrong, and we therefore need to trust our inner voice to reveal to us the right thing to do; (2) that we are free when we decide for ourselves, instead of being influenced by external agencies or authorities; and (3) that each of us is called upon to develop his or her own distinct way to be human.

Taylor (1991) recognises the value of the ideal that he calls 'authenticity' in potentially leading us towards a more responsible way to live. But he also suggests that, in order to perform this function, this ideal needs to be rescued from the extreme subjectivism that we have become used to. In particular, we need to separate it from the false view that moral positions need no justification other than in terms of how we feel. Moral judgements are just the sorts of things that, unlike tastes in food or fashion, do require to be justified in relation to reason and matters of fact. So ideas of what is or is not a good life can be fruitfully discussed with no need for excessive use of the conversation stopper 'Well, that's just your opinion' (Blackburn, 2001, p. 27).

What are the implications of having a theory of the good life? It is by no means the case that having a 'template' needs to result in a uniform recipe for every individual. While it can serve as a rough guide to the good life, such a list is clearly a general one, based on features that human beings share. There are indeed some fairly universal constraints: they are rare people, for instance, who are able to live a good life in the absence of the basics. But people differ in their inclinations, talents and circumstances, and there cannot be a particular balance or unique combination of ingredients that is appropriate for everyone. Both the relative balance of ingredients and the particular way of realising each ingredient may vary between individuals. Not everybody has to fulfil each item, or fulfil it to the same degree. Different individuals could realise each item on the list in different ways. Through the application of practical wisdom we can make the blueprint more concrete by identifying what *for us* is the correct way to fulfil each of the goods and the correct balance of goods.

The next section takes a slight detour from the matter of searching for the ingredients of a flourishing life and considers the vexed issue of the foundations of the good life. Finding a sound way of conceptualising this is important to ground the more practical concerns.

THE FOUNDATIONS OF THE GOOD LIFE

Aristotle's theory that the main purpose for human beings should be to develop their rational nature was grounded in a more general worldview. It was a common belief in the Greece of his time that the universe was rationally ordered and that human beings had a precise place within it. Once this order was understood, the recipe for the good life would follow. This was particularly so in the later Hellenistic philosophy, which was conceived of as a complete system linking scientific and ethical understanding, thus generating a recipe for how to live.

Aristotle's views are encapsulated in the famous 'function argument', according to which everything in the universe has a purpose or function dictated by its essential nature. Just as the purpose of an acorn is to develop into an oak tree, that of human beings is to develop their unique human capacities, in particular their capacity to reason. The function of a thing or creature could be described as 'what it does that makes it what it is' (Nagel, 1980, p. 8), and the good of each thing is specified by its particular function. Human beings do many things, but many of these (nutrition, growth, reproduction, sense perception, movement) are also done by plants and animals, so they are not what makes us human. Since the capacity to reason is what makes us who we are, that is what we should develop in order to have a good life.

There are different interpretations of Aristotle on this. According to a plausible one, it is wrong to think that our distinguishing characteristics *alone* could be suitable ends for complex beings like us: if we removed from our life the features that we have in common with other creatures, we would no longer be describing a *human* life. The good life for us is more likely to be defined by a selective mixture of what we share with other animals and what is distinctive of us.

The function argument has had a bad press. If we are at all of a scientific persuasion (which Aristotle would strongly approve of) we will not be able to take it at face value. Cottingham (1998, p. 10) writes that ever since the birth of science there has been a tension between a goal-directed view of the world, in which everything can be explained in terms of a final cause, and a scientific one, governed by impersonal laws of physics. He reports that in the early seventeenth century Francis Bacon was already asserting that the search for final causes 'is sterile, and, like a virgin consecrated to God, yields no fruit'.

Since then we have had to accept the sad truth that natural processes do not happen for the sake of anything in particular, and goal-directed explanations have been replaced by ones that had seemed counterintuitive before: our development, like that of any other creature, is ruled by the quirks of natural selection and random mutation. In *River out of Eden* (1996, p. 96), Dawkins writes that 'nature is . . . pitilessly indifferent. This is one of the hardest lessons for humans to learn. We cannot admit that things might be neither good nor evil, neither cruel nor kind, but simply callous – indifferent to all suffering, lacking all purpose'.

But adopting a scientific world-view does not mean that our search for the good life is doomed. Perhaps human nature is all we need to support our understanding of human flourishing.

THE QUAGMIRE OF HUMAN NATURE

The concept of human nature could provide a foundation for the good life by revealing that human beings have certain characteristic features that entail that a good life for them must take a particular form (or one of a number of specific forms). But there are some hurdles associated with this kind of project.

The main question is whether there is such a thing as human nature at all. We are very divided in our assessment of human nature. On the one hand, we have become used to a postmodern, relativistic perspective according to which it is not possible to appeal to human nature as a foundation for objective moral judgements because it does not exist. There is no bedrock of humanity, only local practices, and every aspect of human experience is almost entirely shaped by culture. If we took this line, we would be hard pressed to justify any notion of human flourishing or the good human life. At best we could adopt a concept of the good life in relation to particular cultures.

While admitting that our common biology places certain constraints on cultural possibilities, for instance, MacIntyre (1985, p. 161) writes that 'Man without culture is a myth'. He draws attention to the fact that there have been clashing accounts of flourishing and well-being at different times and in different cultures, and that there are 'different and incompatible lists of the virtues; they give a different rank in order of importance to different virtues; and they have different and incompatible theories of the virtues' (p. 181). But while cultural diversity is an important fact about us, there are also facts about us as humans that considerably overlap between cultures.

On the other hand, evolutionary psychology tells us that human nature is alive and well. This has become a fairly stable part of our mental landscape too. But the evolutionary understanding of human nature is open to misinterpretation, and often taken to endorse all sorts of conservative positions, from the fixity of gender roles to the wrongness of homosexuality to the justification of male aggressive and predatory instincts. These conclusions are unwarranted.

In her brilliant *Human Nature after Darwin* (2000), Radcliffe Richards grapples with the question of what the human nature revealed by evolution really implies in terms of what we should or should not do. She explains that evolutionary theory refers to tendencies within species rather than individual behaviour; moreover, it deals with how particular traits have developed, not whether we should welcome and develop these or hold them in check. The fact that love may have originated from some such mechanism as 'I'll scratch your back if you scratch mine' by no means entails that love does not 'really' exist or has no 'real' worth or that we never 'really' love another person. To say that a characteristic is natural from an evolutionary point of view is not to say anything about how things should be: no normative conclusions ensue. Adopting an evolutionary account of human nature, therefore, has no greatly significant consequences for a theory of the good life.

One of the problems is how to decide which of our characteristic features are essential for a flourishing life. As Hurka (1993) points out, human properties are innumerable, and it is simply not possible to develop all of them; also, some of them could not possibly form part of our concept of the good life. 'Humans may be uniquely rational, but they are also the only animals who make fires, despoil the environment, and kill things for fun' (p. 11). Should we view these as important qualities for us to develop?

Indeed, the terrain of this debate is populated by dubious characters such as skilled thieves, gangsters and *mafioso* drug barons, illustrating the point that if we try to equate a good, flourishing life with the development of our distinctive abilities and qualities we do not always get the desired results. Lying and deception are distinctive human characteristics, but most of us would not see these as viable ingredients of the good life. But on what basis do we decide that certain tendencies should be curbed and others encouraged? If we do select some for repression and others for development, we have smuggled values into a definition of human nature that was supposed to *ground* our values, not just *express* them.

BETWEEN GODS AND BEASTS

If science will not provide the answers, where does this leave us? Hursthouse (1999) reports that Foot begins one of her papers with the – seemingly surprising – remark that in moral philosophy it is useful to think about plants. The strategy adopted by Foot and endorsed by Hursthouse is to argue that, just as plants and animals can be evaluated as good or bad specimens of their kind, so must humans. Just as ' "there is something wrong with a free-riding wolf, who eats but does not take part in the hunt" and "with a member of the species of dancing bees who finds a source of nectar but does not let other bees know where it is", there is something wrong with a human being who lacks, for example, charity and justice' (p. 196).

What might be the human equivalent of a free-riding wolf or a secretive bee? We have already seen that the answer is not to be found in the presence or absence of particular tendencies identified by evolutionary theory, since these would be non-normative. Hursthouse (1999) writes that, unlike other animals, we are not wholly constrained by our inherited past: apart from obvious physical and perhaps psychological limitations, we are able to assess the way we are and at least try to change it: if it is natural that female cheetahs have a worse life than male cheetahs, female human beings do not have to accept any such notions of what is 'natural'.

She concludes that there *is* something characteristic of human beings, but not in the same way as other animals: while typical animal behaviours (such as food acquisition, mating, rearing the young) have to be described in detailed terms and are discovered by observation, the one truly characteristic feature of human beings is that we are able to act from reasons as opposed to slavishly following our instincts and desires. The fact that we are able to do this at all connects with the earlier suggestion that the good life for humans may consist mainly in activity according to reason. But clearly we do not always act from *good* reasons, and therefore proficient rational activity should be seen as an ethical ideal rather than as a value-free description.

Perhaps then the project should take a different form, dropping the scientific aim of justifying ethical principles on the basis of neutral features and adopting instead the aim of producing a specification of the good life that is based on our most profound sense of what it means to be a human being. According to Nussbaum (1994, p. 61), for instance, the good human life 'must, in the first place, be such that a human being *can* live it'.

Nussbaum has developed this normative account in a couple of important papers (1993, 1995). Her main point is that the good *human* life has to be defined in relation to what humans – not gods or beasts – would find plausible. The question of what a good human life is cannot be answered from an external, scientific perspective, since it necessarily has to connect with beliefs about aspects of our existence that are so central as to be defining of who we are, and without which our life could not be said to be human. According to Isaiah Berlin, ends 'must be within the human horizon' and 'cannot be unlimited, for the nature of men, however various and subject to change, must possess some generic character if it is to be called human at all' (cited in Rasmussen, 1999, p. 40).

Nussbaum's (1993) 'take' on the Aristotelian virtues is that they are related to spheres of human experience that tend to occur in everybody's life and that it is not really possible for us as human beings to avoid. Aristotle's question then is: 'What is it to choose and respond well in that sphere? And what is it to choose defectively?' (p. 245). These spheres of experience are related to such fundamental issues as death, the body, pleasure and pain, and social interactions, and present most of us with difficult choices: 'The question about virtue usually arises in areas in which human choice is both non-optional and somewhat problematic. Each family of virtue and vice . . . attaches to some such sphere' (p. 248).

A MARRIAGE OF OBJECTIVITY AND PLURALISM

A scientific notion of human nature will not help us to construct an ideal of the good life because it will not tell us which characteristics to cultivate and which to curb. But there is still much that human nature can do for us by illuminating the boundaries of human flourishing, the areas of choice that as humans we cannot avoid negotiating, and the qualities and virtues required to do that well.

The constraints imposed by human nature stem from the fact that as a result of being particular kinds of creatures human beings have certain general needs – to do with food, shelter, community, freedom from extreme pain, and a certain amount of liberty and autonomy – in the absence of which flourishing is unlikely. Kekes (1988) identifies a number of physiological, psychological and social facts that create minimum standards to which good lives must conform. A common criticism is that although we can in this way establish minimal qualifying constraints (entry qualifications, as it were) on the notion of a good life, beyond this things become a little more indeterminate.

But we are beings that can reflect and reason. If this capacity is removed from our life, it will no longer be the life of a human: '[t]he mindless life is not ruled out by external facts of nature; . . . what is established is the cost of the choice, and how deeply it is at odds with some of our firmest convictions concerning who we are' (Nussbaum, 1995, p. 117). The conclusion that the good life for us has to involve the use of reason does not dictate any particular way of realising this, but it does reduce the number of possible good lives, eliminating for example a life given totally and exclusively to passive pleasures.

Practical wisdom is exercised in connection with the basic facts of human life. It is because of our mortality, bodily needs, dependence on the world outside us, pain and pleasure, desires and appetites that practical wisdom is called for. It is the whole package that defines our experience, creating commonality and overlap across the variety of human cultural expressions. But this does not give us anything like a precise recipe for how to conduct our life. As Rasmussen (1999, p. 6) puts it: 'The generic goods and virtues of human flourishing are not like Recommended Daily Allowances for vitamins and minerals. Their weighting, balance, or proportion cannot be read off human nature like the back of a cereal box and applied equally across all individuals as if individuals were merely repositories for the generic goods and virtues. Rather, it is only when the individual's particular talents, potentialities, and circumstances are jointly engaged that these goods and virtues become real or achieve determinacy.'

The fact that beyond basic requirements our recipe for the good life becomes vague does not mean that any judgements and evaluations are just as good as any others. It only means that we need to reflect on how the notion of the good life is to apply to our own case, given our particular temperament and circumstances. Nussbaum (1993, p. 257) uses an enlightening analogy with navigation: 'Aristotelian particularism is fully compatible with Aristotelian objectivity. The fact that a good and virtuous decision is context-sensitive does not imply that it is right only *relative to*, or *inside* a limited context, any more than the fact that a good navigational judgement is sensitive to particular weather conditions shows that it is correct only in a local or relational sense.'

An ideal of the good life, then, can be objective in the sense of involving certain ingredients and ruling out others on the basis of the kind of creatures we are. At the same time, however, it can be agent-relative in the sense that there is no exact specification of the balance of ingredients or how each ingredient is to be realised. As Isaiah Berlin wrote: 'The general parameters of human flourishing are provided by human nature. Their concrete form is not' (cited in Rasmussen, 1999, p. 40). Concrete questions can be resolved only in relation to particular situations and individuals.

An Aristotelian approach allows the moral agent to determine the right course of action in relation to particular facts as well as general principles, foregoing rigid and inflexible rules such as 'thou shalt' and 'thou shalt not' (Grayling, 2003, p. 29). It is just because precision is not to be sought in the sphere of human affairs – as Aristotle always warned – that this is such a rich area to explore in counselling and psychotherapy.

PRACTICAL APPLICATIONS

A basic fact of life is that we have ideals and desires – sometimes a wealth of them – and limited powers to achieve them during lives of limited duration. Given this, developing *all* our human abilities to the full is simply not an option. Devoting all our energies to one goal is likely to mean that others will suffer, and this may or may not be an acceptable outcome. According to Russell (1975), 'In the good life there must be a balance between different activities, and no one of them must be carried so far as to make the others impossible' (p. 128). But he qualifies this by saying that '[a]s a limitation upon the doctrine that has just been set forth, it ought to be admitted that some performances are considered so essentially noble as to justify the sacrifice of everything else on their behalf' (p. 129).

Goals and ideals may clash, either intrinsically or because there are too many of them. In these imperfect circumstances, we need to think through which to adopt, to what extent to pursue them, and how to reconcile them with other goals and ideals. Doing this will make it less likely that we turn back at the end of our life and, like Tolstoy's Ivan Ilyich, realise when it is too late that we have squandered our time on ultimately trivial or inappropriate activities. There is no right balance of ingredients that does not make reference to individuals. Most people have talents and skills in some areas but are lacking in others.

Depending on our particular combination of capacities and their relative importance, we may choose to devote substantial time and effort to developing the areas in which we are not well endowed, or instead accept our limitations and give greater emphasis to the areas in which we are.

There are many possible clashes of goals and ideals: deep personal relationships and family life, for instance, may clash with a life of contemplation or dedication to art, research or a social or political cause. These ideals are not intrinsically contradictory, but because of limitations of time and energy we may find ourselves in the position of having to choose between them or rank them in order of importance.

A tension that is often present in people's lives is that between achievement and contentment. Both of these seem genuine goods, well worth developing: devoting time and energy to a well-chosen goal and seeing the results of our efforts is an important part of the good life, just as never straying from our comfort zone is likely to be ultimately unsatisfactory. At the same time, however, exclusive concentration on achievement can be hollow and make for a stressful life. And the capacity to accept our lot and be content with what we have is also a crucial part of the good life. It may be possible for us to have both, in which case we need to learn when to prioritise achievement and when instead well-being and a peaceful state of mind. Or it may be that one of these poles is so important to us that we are prepared to all intents and purposes to give the other up and to live with the consequences.

Similarly, there is a possible tension between the variety of a well-rounded life and dedication to one activity. The two horns of this dilemma have been called *dilettante's disadvantage* and *costs of concentration* (Hurka, 1993). On the one hand, it is often the case that the more we invest in an activity, the more we gain from it. Trying to do too many things may lead to 'spreading ourselves thin' and only skimming the surface of each. On the other hand, if we devote all our time and energy to one activity we run the risk of having a narrow life and missing out on richness of experience. Should we prioritise depth and high achievement or breadth and a well-rounded life? Each will entail a substantial sacrifice, but for most of us something has to give.

As has been discussed, while human nature may reveal a plurality of generic goods and virtues, this does nothing towards specifying the relative importance of these for particular individuals, or how any particular individual would be best advised to pursue any one of them. As Rasmussen (1999, p. 14) puts it, 'what human flourishing amounts to in terms of concrete activities for any particular individual is not something that can be simply read off human nature in some recipe-like manner'. Similarly, Nussbaum (1994, p. 67) writes that: 'Excellent ethical choice cannot be captured completely in general rules because – like medicine – it is a matter of fitting one's choice to the complex requirements of a concrete situation, taking all of its contextual features into account.' This is why practical wisdom is so crucial. Since there are no rules dictating the universal balance or weighting of goods and virtues, this task has to be carried out with reference to each situation. But there is no algorithm available to perform this calculation; so it is important to learn to balance general principles with an acute and accurate understanding of particular situations.

It is worth reiterating the point that practical wisdom is both a means to an end and an end in itself. Learning to negotiate and choose in all these dilemmas is, to the extent that it involves the use of practical wisdom, already a way of living by reason. Whether we choose to prioritise devotion to a worthy pursuit or family life, peace of mind or achievement, a life of balance or a single-minded pursuit of one ingredient, using practical wisdom in the process is part and parcel of the good life.

This thinking through should be done in the light of our knowledge of ourselves and the world, of what is possible and desirable for a particular individual in a particular corner of the world at a particular time. What should be considered in this respect is 'the set of circumstances, talents, endowments, interests, beliefs, and histories that descriptively characterize the individual – what . . . [could be called] his or her "nexus" – as well as the individual's community and culture' (Rasmussen, 1999, p. 14).

But sometimes we run into difficulties and need extra help in clarifying, in identifying priorities or in disentangling limitations from possibilities. As has already been pointed out, many people end up in psychotherapists' consulting rooms in the attempt to answer that fundamental question: 'Am I satisfied with my life as a whole?' – to find meaning and purpose, to live well. What a therapist can do then is to help clients to reflect on the good life in general and in particular, to assess the relative importance of goals and ideals, the appropriate balance of ingredients, or the best way to achieve any particular ingredient. This should be done in relation to the client's temperament and abilities as well as to the circumstances and possibilities that the world offers.

The themes to reflect on at this stage are those that will help clients to gain insight into what matters in life and to make links between values and ideals on the one hand and concrete goals on the other. The initial step in this process is to enquire about the clients' world-view and actual values. There are many ways to pursue this line of enquiry, and many available resources (see, for instance, Crumbaugh, 1973, and LeBon, 2001). Here is a selection of questions that may prove useful in helping to elicit this information:

- What would you regret if looking back over your life from your deathbed?
- What are the main values that unreflectively come to mind?
- Whom do you admire, and why?
- What have been your most valuable experiences, and why?
- What is your 'ideal life' fantasy?
- Which daily activities are means to ends and which are ends in themselves?

Some forms of counselling and life coaching use similar exercises to clarify clients' goals. But the answers to the above questions should be seen as providing only *clues* to value, and should be probed and examined rather than passively accepted. After generating initial values, clients should be helped to explore:

- whether those values withstand scrutiny
- the *relative* importance of values and ideals
- the extent to which these are currently being realised
- any clashes between values
- the reality of the circumstances
- talents, abilities and inclinations
- whether in practice life goals match values and ideals
- how conflicts can be resolved
- how choices can be made
- any gains and losses resulting from these.

Reflecting on ideals and connecting them to reality is the first step in helping clients in their search for the good life. Other essential pieces of the jigsaw are: cultivating practical wisdom and the virtues of character, managing emotions and developing self-control. These will be covered in the chapters that follow.

2

Practical Wisdom: The Art of Making Good Decisions

Decision-making is not easy. In *The Unbearable Lightness of Being* (1985, p. 8) Kundera perceptively points out that 'We can never know what to want, because, living only one life, we can neither compare it with our previous lives nor perfect it in our lives to come'. It is indeed impossible for us to experiment with different courses of action in order to select the one that turns out to be most satisfactory. It is part of the human predicament to have to make choices in conditions of ignorance and uncertainty.

While not many clients are likely explicitly to consult a therapist with a view to developing practical wisdom, they may do so because they have trouble with decision-making: they find it difficult to arrive at a decision at all, or often change their minds, or make decisions and fail to act on them. Decision-making can certainly be hard work, and undoubtedly features among the most common client issues.

THE DICE MAN

An extreme response to the relentless necessity to choose is heroically to refuse to rise to the challenge. This was the paradoxical approach chosen by the Dice Man (Rhinehart, 1999). The Dice Man was a bored psychiatrist, going through what could be described as a midlife crisis, who on a whim one night decided to let a pair of dice dictate whether he should go back to bed to his wife or instead rape his downstairs neighbour. Rape is decreed, and our hero goes on to develop a fully-fledged dice life, his search for randomness becoming more and more extreme until it leads to the almost complete disintegration of the texture of his life and eventually to murder.

There is something morbidly fascinating about the Dice Man. These are his after-rape thoughts:

> Rape had been possible for years, decades even, but was realized only when I stopped looking at whether it were possible, or prudent, or even desirable, but without premeditation did it, feeling myself a puppet to a force outside me, a creature of the gods – the die – rather than a responsible agent. The cause was chance or fate, not me. The probability of that die being a one was only one in six. The chance of the die's being there under the card, maybe one in a million. My rape was obviously dictated by fate. Not guilty.
>
> (p. 74)

His life project becomes that of transforming himself from a responsible agent who does things for reasons to someone who does things randomly. There is something faintly inhuman about this, and of course the process is somewhat incompatible with normal life commitments – jobs, relationships, perhaps even basic human interactions.

> Now the dice treated everything and everyone as objects and forced me to do the same. The emotions I was to feel for all things were determined by the dice and not by the intrinsic relationship between me and the person or thing. Love I saw as an irrational, arbitrary relationship to another object. It was compulsive. It was an important part of the historical self. It must be destroyed.
>
> (p. 118)

He resolves to let the dice decide his long-term fate:

> I wrote with unfirm hand and dazed eyes the first option, for snake-eyes or double-sixes: I would leave my wife and children and begin a separate life. I trembled . . . and felt proud. Sooner or later the dice would roll a two or a twelve and the last great test of the dice's ability to destroy the self would occur. If I left Lil there would be no turning back: it would be dice unto death.
>
> (p. 172)

The Dice Man is something of a paradox: even though his project rebels against the most fundamental sense of being human, of being an agent, he does nevertheless *have* a life project, and given this rather unusual project of his the steps he takes in order to realise it are nothing but rational. If randomness was what he wanted, he did all the right things to achieve it as far as humanly possible. The options given to the dice were of course still controlled by an agent, but one who was positively trying to come up with options that did not relate to a consistent pattern of beliefs and desires, or even to anything he desired at all – apart, clearly, from randomness itself.

This is the Dice Man's manifesto:

> In theory, we're working toward the purely random man, one without habit or pattern, eating from zero to six or seven times a day, sleeping haphazardly, responding sexually randomly to men, women, dogs, elephants, trees, watermelons, snails and so on. In practice, of course, we don't shoot so high.
>
> (p. 323)

In the end any semblance of normality drains from his life, and a fellow psychiatrist quietly concludes: 'the man is no longer human' (p. 332).

CAN WE RELATE TO THE DICE MAN'S LIFE PROJECT?

1. Sometimes the Dice Man's aspiration to destroy his sense of self appears to connect with certain religious ideas, particularly from Buddhism, about the illusory nature of the self, and then for a while we warm to him and think we understand. But then the feeling of 'alienness' returns. There are dangers in taking religious and philosophical ideas too literally: there may well be no solid self, but unless we take care in crossing the road there will not be a 'self' left to contemplate metaphysical truths. To the extent that the Dice Man's project is inspired by a spiritual quest, it is cut off from that context and taken to self-destructive extremes.

2. Another aspect of the Dice Man's project that we can superficially relate to is his rejection of habit and routine, his search for freshness of experience. But the similarity is only apparent: our commendable desire for spontaneity and variety is still the desire of an agent with a more or less integrated pattern of plans, beliefs and desires. Spontaneity is valuable, but not at the cost of losing everything else.

3. We can also relate to the Dice Man in terms of the common and occasionally useful practice of tossing a coin. But living by this decision-making method is not easy: when I tried it, the first stumbling-block was the fact that I was not prepared to let the dice handle all my decisions, such as whether I should go to work ('the dice told me not to' is an interesting reason in a novel, but not much

of an excuse in real life). And I did not want to risk having to give up my plans. I could conceive of using the dice for trivial options, such as, on a weekend away, deciding what streets to explore, or when and where to have lunch. But this seemed pointless. I suspect that in real life random outcomes are acceptable only when the choice is unimportant and/or the options are equally attractive (or unattractive), which are indeed the situations in which we might toss a coin. A long way from the Dice Man.

ARISTOTLE AND THE DICE MAN

What has the Dice Man to do with Aristotle and the virtues? A lot, in the sense that an agent who has chosen randomness as a primary goal is in many ways the opposite of an Aristotelian agent. From an Aristotelian point of view, the ideal of doing things at random is wrong, as it implies a rejection of the fundamentally human position of being an agent who acts for reasons and is willing and able to take responsibility for his or her actions. It also implies the rejection of other things that matter in a good life, such as meaningful relationships. On the other hand, as I pointed out earlier, the Dice Man is a model example of means–end reasoning: he aimed for randomness, and randomness he achieved, even if it predictably led to his own destruction. (Or did it? The end of the book is somewhat enigmatic. But we can probably assume that it would.)

Let us remind ourselves that Aristotle divides reason into *theoretical* (*sophia*) and *practical* (*phronêsis*). Having practical reason, or wisdom, means not just being able to take the necessary steps to achieve our goals, but also to act on the best available reasons and select the course of action that is most likely to lead to as flourishing and fulfilled a life as is attainable in the circumstances. The Dice Man clearly succeeded at the former but failed at the latter. Doing things for reasons is the central requirement of being a human agent, and that is why the project of randomness is likely to undermine our very humanity. According to Aristotle, the main mark of practical wisdom is *good deliberation*.

GOOD DELIBERATION

After reflection on the values and ideals conducive to the good life (see Chapter 1) comes the ability to put our principles into practice in particular situations. The values that tend to lead to flourishing are like generalised headings and do not give us a clear indication of what we should concretely aim for in life, therefore we need to make that understanding specific and practical. This involves linking our general insights about what really matters in life with the particular situations we find ourselves in.

Aristotle illustrates this point with a metaphor about health:

> For if someone knew that light meats are digestible and wholesome, but did not know which kinds are light, he would not produce health; rather, the person who knows that chicken is wholesome will be better at producing health. And since practical wisdom is practical, one needs both kinds of knowledge, but especially the particular kind.
>
> (*NE*, Book VI, Ch. 7)

If we know that light meats are healthy, but do not know which meats are light, we will not be able to adopt a healthy diet. Similarly, we could come up with a vague description of something we want:

> a good life, a satisfying profession, an interesting holiday, an amusing evening – and the problem is . . . to see what really *qualifies* as an adequate and practically realizable specification of what would satisfy this want. Deliberation is . . . a search for the *best specification*.
>
> (Wiggins, 1980, p. 228)

We may know that one of our important guiding principles is to help people, for instance. The question then arises as to how we should put this into practice. We could choose to become doctors, priests, psychotherapists, campaigners for Amnesty International or one of many other things that could more or less legitimately fall under that umbrella. Having practical wisdom means that we will be able to select the goals that are most appropriate to our situation, given our talents, inclinations, skills and opportunities.

Or we may believe that kindness is a good thing. In practice, however, it is by no means always obvious what the kind course of action is, especially in the trickier sorts of situations, when we need to be able to make good action-guiding judgements informed by sound values. Asked by an aspiring writer for an opinion on his or her first novel, which we happen to consider unviable, we need:

> the ability to discern in this particular instance whether saying 'This will never sell' would be an act of kindness or an unsympathetic lack of encouragement to a nervous beginner. The ability to discern in this way

requires . . . knowing both that now is a time for kindness, and what it would be kind to say here and now.

(Hughes, 2001, p. 101)

REASONS FOR ACTION

The possibilities and constraints of human decision-making may be better appreciated by considering circumstances in which it is not an issue. One extreme is the fantasy of ideal rationality. We can just about imagine a being who has perfect understanding of all the relevant features of a given situation, of what considerations should be decisive in relation to it, and of the consequences of different courses of actions. This creature would be more like a god than a human being. We can surmise that decisions for him or her would not present the difficulties they create for us, who are in the unenviable position of constantly having to choose from within a fog of ignorance and delusion.

The other extreme is that of no rationality. Non-human animals are not known for endlessly pondering difficult decisions. We may fancy a cat weighing up the pros and cons of chasing a bird, but that is only if we are looking through cartoon-like anthropomorphic spectacles. In reality we know that animal behaviour is dictated by instinct as opposed to careful reflection on the situation at hand. Dennett (2003) writes about *degrees of freedom*. Yes, birds can fly wherever they want and have a degree of freedom compared with amoebas, but their 'choices' are regulated by 'the settings of all the switches in the brain' (p. 164). They do not ask themselves questions about where it might be best to winter this year.

Human minds, on the other hand, are 'furnished – and beset – by thousands of anticipations, evaluations, projects, schemes, hopes, fears, and memories that are entirely inaccessible to the minds of even our closest relatives, the great apes. This world of human ideals and artefacts gives individual human beings capacities and proclivities that are strikingly different from those of any other living beings on the planet' (Dennett, 2003, p. 143). Through language, we are able to ask: 'What should I do?' We are able to consider possible answers and reflect on the conceivable ramifications and likely advantages or disadvantages of different courses of action.

All the time, whether we realise it or not, we are challenged to find an answer to the following question: 'All things considered, what is the best course of action for this individual in this situation?' And the core of the answer is to be found in the notion of doing things for *reasons*.

We are able to detect value in the world, and as a result we come to care for certain things and states of affairs. Blackburn (1998) calls these our *concerns*. This leads to the existence of reasons to act in order to secure the things or states of affairs that we have come to see as valuable. In this process, our consciousness is crowded by a mixed bag of concerns: some self-interested, some altruistic, some to do with short-term gratification, some with our long-term future.

In order to qualify as rational agents at all, we need to be able to connect our reasons with our actions in some way. But doing this well is not easy, and the process can be fraught with obstacles. We are besieged by all sorts of competing motives and considerations. We have only a tenuous grasp of their relevance to the situation and their importance relative to each other. We are largely ignorant of potential future implications and interconnections. We have to act on pitifully limited information. Normally the strongest concern at the time wins and – for better or for worse – a decision just emerges.

What can it mean therefore to make a rational decision? It has been pointed out (Raz, 1999) that the term 'rational' can refer to both (1) our capacity to indentify reasons for action and respond to them, and (2) the competent use of this ability. If we lack the former (as in the case of non-human animals), we are beyond rationality or irrationality; if we are lacking in relation to the latter we may be described as irrational. Using this capacity well means being able to (1) sift, from the array of reasons for plunging down one road or another, those that point to options of real value for us, (2) choose a course of action from this subset of reasons and (3) act on it. Using it badly could mean being unable to identify the reasons that point to real value, or not acting on them.

The main problem is that our perception of value is subjective and may be deluded: some things in the world are actually better and some worse for us (as human beings and as individuals), but our judgement on this may be mistaken. If we want to develop practical wisdom we need to learn to identify the reasons for action that are based on sound concerns, on things that really are good for us, and act on them. We need to act on our *best all-things-considered judgement* rather than – unthinkingly – on our strongest motive.

Dissecting the Question

Let us take a closer look at the different components of the question: *all things considered, what is the best course of action for this individual in this situation?*

All things considered: We often have difficulties with decisions because we want different things that seem to conflict with each other. There is an important distinction that needs to be made here between two senses of 'want'. The first sense is about *motivation*, feeling inclined or desiring to do something; the second involves a *judgement* that something is good for us, or in our interest, or the right thing to do (Watson, 1977). These two types of want can clash. An 'all things considered' decision is made on the basis of a careful assessment of both (Davidson, 1980).[4] The kinds of considerations that are relevant in this respect are any reasons in favour of and against a course of action and their relative importance: in particular, how strong an inclination is and whether it would be harmful to follow it, what our judgement is based on (duties, obligations, assessment of consequences) and whether on reflection we endorse it.

Best: How are we to put our wants in some kind of hierarchical order? Faced with an army of reasons in favour of or against a particular course of action, we need to have some way of assessing them. If the decision is particularly important, we may begin with a list of pros and cons to help us to think things through. But this is not enough: what is needed is a winnowing out of the *good reasons* from *bad reasons* and *excuses*. This is another important distinction to bear in mind. We should examine each of our reasons through the lens of critical thinking so as to be able to decide whether to stand by them or discard them.

This individual: It is important to think clearly about ourselves, reflecting on what we really are like rather than what we wish we were like, or have been like, or are used to thinking we are like.

This situation: We also need to think clearly about the situation, identifying the features that are most relevant to our decision and realistically considering what can or cannot be changed, constraints and opportunities.

Our decision-making is likely to be improved if, before deciding, we:

- identify all reasons (including judgements, emotions and desires);
- critically assess them – distinguishing good and bad reasons, separating valid reasons from self-deceived ones, working out if our

---

[4]As Dennett (1984) points out, 'it would be insane to consider all things' (p. 70). No matter how much we reflect and evaluate, we could always do more. So we may have to read 'all-things-considered' as something like: 'once we have surveyed as many relevant considerations as possible in the circumstances'.

emotions are providing a clue to real value or simply distorting our judgement;
- roughly order them by importance.

Examples and Reflections

A. Greg is worried about his drinking and is considering giving it up. (It may or may not be possible for Greg to reduce his alcohol intake, but I shall simplify the scenario by assuming that this is not a realistic goal for him.) His reasons for giving up are:

- he is concerned about his health;
- he has come to realise that drinking stops him spending time on creative and artistic pursuits, which he considers more valuable;
- he does not like the fact that he has become psychologically dependent on alcohol and uses it to relieve uncomfortable feelings like anxiety and boredom.

His reasons for continuing to drink are:

- he would miss the sociable aspect of it;
- the habit is very engrained, and breaking it is likely to require a major effort;
- he is not sure he would be able to learn to deal with unpleasant feelings without the mellowing effect of alcohol.

There is a sense in which Greg wants both to continue to drink and to stop drinking. Wanting to continue means that he is *motivated* to continue (he enjoys it and is used to it), and wanting to stop means that he has formed a *judgement* to the effect that stopping would be good for him in a number of ways. At the moment, the two senses of 'want' are clashing: his habit-driven inclination is winning, but he is becoming more and more concerned about it. What should Greg do? He should critically assess each reason in order to decide how important it is in his life and whether he wants to stand by it. Having assessed potential gains and losses in this way, he should come to an overall judgement about what to do. In other words, continuing to drink simply because he feels like it is probably not the wisest course of action. On the other hand, the fact that there are good reasons to give up does not automatically mean that this is the best overall judgement: his motivation – the reasons for continuing – should be carefully considered first.

Greg should realistically assess the effort required in order to alter the habits of a lifetime and to find alternative ways to deal with negative feelings, and only then commit himself to a goal. The desire to drink will not magically disappear, and doubts are likely to creep in when it starts making itself felt again: thoughts to the effect that perhaps he does not really want to give up after all, that it is too difficult and he does not need the stress right now, that he cannot tolerate this anxiety, that he just needs a drink and so on. If Greg has come to a sound decision, having considered all factors, then he will be more able to identify such thoughts as self-deceived and argue them down. But if he has not thought things through enough, he may well take these thoughts seriously and rapidly change his mind about his goal.

In the above vignette, the reasons to give up appeared stronger than the ones to continue. In particular, the fact that a change requires effort and the learning of new behaviours would not in itself seem a good reason against the change. If, however, we alter the scenario to one in which the reasons for giving up are altogether less compelling (perhaps Greg is not drinking that much, and the negative effects on his health are not likely to be that significant; drinking does not stop Greg pursuing the artistic and creative activities that matter to him; his social life is overwhelmingly important to him, and tends to involve drinking; his main reason to give up is that he wants to see if he can do it), the best overall judgement may indeed be that it is not worth putting a huge amount of energy and effort into this change.

B. Lauren is thinking of running a marathon for charity, but she is wavering and wants to be sure that it is a good idea before she commits herself.

Possible reasons in favour:

- she wants to get fit;
- she wants to raise money for the charity;
- she wants to prove to herself that she can do it;
- her ex-partner did it last year, and she wants to show him that she can do it too.

Possible reasons against:

- she is not very fit at the moment, and does not know whether physically she could cope with it;
- the training will interfere with her busy work schedule;

- the training will reduce the already limited time she can spend with her children;
- she has a knee condition that could be made worse by it.

Let us look at different balances of reasons. If, for instance, all the reasons against it hold, and her main reason to do it is that she wants to show her ex-partner, the balance of reasons would seem to be on the side of not doing it. Instead, Lauren should examine why it seems so important to show her ex-partner, and whether she really wants to risk serious harm to pursue this goal. Of course there are situations in which we commit ourselves to courses of action that are not ultimately in our overall best interest but favour a limited and partial set of reasons, such as a strong desire for revenge. This may be altered by a thorough exploration of the desire, the possible consequences of acting on it, the losses it would entail – which should be imagined vividly – and consideration of whether we really are prepared to lose everything else to satisfy it.

On the other hand, if Lauren's main reasons in favour are that she wants to get fit and raise money for charity, and the main reason against is the worry about not being fit enough, it may be that this is borne out of fear of doing something new and challenging – after all, she can become fit enough with training. The process of thinking through and sifting reasons involves looking at each of these and their overall balance before we can draw a final conclusion about what is likely to be best all things considered. If there is any ambivalence to begin with, the opposite set of reasons can be expected to make itself felt again at some point, and it is only if the deliberation process has been thorough that we are likely to be able to spot bad reasons and excuses and deal with them.

A couple of asides are in order here:

1. The right thing for us in a situation need not be equated with the sensible thing. We may want to undertake a dangerous physical feat that will have serious consequences if it goes wrong. The mountaineer Alison Hargreaves, who died descending from K2 in 1995, was criticised for her choice to risk her life climbing, which eventually meant that her children were deprived of their mother at an early age. Without knowing the details of any situation it is wise to suspend judgement, but we can conceive of goals that are so overwhelmingly central within someone's life that he or she is truly prepared to risk everything for them. Some pursuits, however, seem to

be more appropriate candidates for this kind of choice than others: exploration, or welfare, or research, perhaps, rather than drinking oneself to death.

2. This process can be hard work, and it would not be rational to give every decision this much thought. It is only when decisions are momentous and involve many contradictory reasons that we may want to allocate the time and effort to go through them. We should train ourselves to avoid giving too much attention to small daily choices such as what film to see or what supermarket to use on a given occasion. Of course such decisions may *turn out* to be momentous – serendipitously, we may meet the love of our life in the cinema queue, or be run over by a bus on the way to the supermarket. But these are totally unforeseeable factors and therefore should not be included in our deliberation.

SKILLS AND ABILITIES

The following skills and abilities seem essential to be able to choose wisely between alternative courses of action:

- a correct understanding of what is possible;
- a correct understanding of ourselves and the situation;
- awareness of self-deception;
- critical thinking;
- selecting the right steps towards our goals.

Understanding What is Possible

According to Aristotle, there is no point in deliberating about certain things at all:

> No one deliberates about eternal things, such as the universe, or the fact that the diagonal is incommensurable with the side; nor things that involve movement but always happen in the same way, either from necessity or by nature or through some other cause, such as the solstices or the rising of the stars; nor things that happen now in one way, now in another, such as droughts and rains; nor what happens by chance, such as the finding of treasure. We do not deliberate even about all human affairs; no Spartan, for example, would deliberate about the best form of government for the Scythians. The reason is that we could not bring about any of these things.
>
> (*NE*, Book III, Ch. 3)

We should deliberate only about what is in our power to change: 'What is possible is what can be accomplished by our own efforts' (*NE*, Book III, Ch. 3). We should not deliberate about things that are impossible to achieve, either for any human being (like changing the past, or being immortal) or for us in particular. The Serenity Prayer encapsulates this:

'God, grant me the courage to change the things that I can change, the serenity to accept the things that I cannot change, and the wisdom to know the difference.'

Of course the judgement about whether something is or is not possible for us as individuals might be substantially harder to make than whether we can bring dead people back to life. There is a heroic school of thought, ever present in self-help books and some counselling and life-coaching circles, according to which we all have unlimited potential and can do anything we choose if only we put our mind to it and are sufficiently positive-thinking. This is not the case. There are very real limitations in life that we had better pay attention to. It is no longer possible for me to become a ballet dancer. For anyone of a nervous disposition, being an astronaut might not be a great career choice. The same goes for a career in politics if we are basically shy and reserved, or choosing to become war correspondents if we are risk averse.

Some of these choices may not be strictly impossible, but we should be aware of the costs of pushing ourselves so far out of our comfort zone as to create real tension in our life. It is also important to know when to give up our goals if we become faced with impossibility. We should avoid both giving up too soon and doggedly persevering once it has become clear that a particular goal is likely to be beyond our reach.

Understanding Ourselves and the Situation

Unless we are clear about our particular inclinations, dispositions, strengths and weaknesses and about what the circumstances really offer us, we will not be able to make wise choices.

Consider the case of a newly-graduated doctor who is hesitating between becoming a Peace Corps volunteer in a developing country and a junior partner in a lucrative private practice in a large American city. One day she feels inclined to the former path, seeing herself as an idealistic person who is altruistic, dedicated, socially committed, and unconcerned with material comforts. The next day she feels inclined to the other path, seeing herself in more conventional terms as a successful, respected, career-oriented professional. Her hesitation may be described as a hesitation between two ways of life, both of which will shape her future self in different ways. In both cases she is healing the sick, and therefore realising some of the primary aims of her life-plan. But ... [e]ach course of action involves realising diverging fundamental life-possibilities.

(Jopling, 1996, p. 304)

What does this doctor need to do in order to deliberate well? She needs to assess and order her reasons in order to come to a sound judgement about which option is, all things considered, better suited to her personality and circumstances. It is not the case that any choice is as good a match as any other, and lack of self-understanding could lead us to make unrealistic decisions that do not reflect our true psychological and moral make-up. Undoubtedly there are many facets to our personalities and multiple legitimate self-descriptions, so there may be occasions when we simply need to choose which of these we wish to develop at a particular time. But even this depends on self-knowledge, since it requires an understanding of our relative priorities at that time.

The doctor may want adventure in her life, but also home comforts and a close relationship with her family. If our goals seem to clash we need to decide whether they are intrinsically incompatible (in which case we have to choose which is more valuable and which to give up) or whether it is possible to satisfy more than one (immediately or in the long term). In this case, even though the goals may not be inherently incompatible, there may be no available option that fulfils all of them neatly (so it could be that one option satisfies the need for adventure and another the need for home comforts, but no option satisfies both equally at the same time). But there is still the option of reconsidering how to achieve an ideal: it may be possible, for instance, to find alternative ways of bringing more adventure into life that would not clash with other values.

Self-knowledge and understanding of the situation should also inform the *level* of our goals: if this is too low, our life will be boring and unfulfilling; if too high, it is likely to be anxious and tense. According to *flow* theory (Csikszentmihalyi, 1992), a goal is pitched at the right level when our skills and the challenges we face are well matched, when we are stretched and have the opportunity to develop our skills but do not feel totally overwhelmed by the task.

We must remember, however, that there can be too much of a good thing: self-knowledge should be balanced between the extremes of self-obsessed navel-gazing and complete ignorance of our own motivations, dispositions and talents. As has been said, 'The unexamined life may not be worth living, but the overexamined life is nothing to write home about either' (cited in Dennett, 1984, p. 87).

Self-deception

Knowing ourselves involves guarding against self-deception. An awareness of the mechanisms involved should help us to do this, as should the critical thinking strategies suggested in the next section.

There is something paradoxical about self-deception, yet it is clearly a common human experience. The reason for the paradox is that we tend to construe self-deception on the model of interpersonal deception, which typically involves intentionally getting someone to believe something that we know to be false. Applying this to one and the same person, we get the picture not only that X is deceived in believing that something is the case, but also that X has *intentionally* executed this deception. But how could this be? If we believe that something is false, how can we at the same time try to get ourselves to believe it is true?

Traditionally, the problem has been 'solved' by positing some kind of inner duality. If we have two distinct subsystems within the self-deceiver, then one can play the role of deceiver and the other of deceived, and in this way we avoid a situation in which a single subject believes and does not believe the same thing at the same time. A well-known strategy in this respect is the psychoanalytic one of dividing the agent into a conscious and an unconscious part, separated by a 'censor' whose function it is to decide which unconscious desires and instincts are to be allowed into consciousness. On this understanding, what happens when we deceive ourselves is that the censor admits a belief into consciousness that the censor itself knows to be false.

This view of self-deception was criticised by Sartre (1958), who pointed out the paradox of positing one and the same person as deceiver and deceived, knowing and not knowing something at the same time. Sartre commented that in this strategy the paradox, far from being solved, is simply shifted to a different level. The censor, in fact, must somehow be conscious of the drives in order not to be conscious of them, which still means that a person is aware and not aware of the same thing at the same time. So the appeal to a dual consciousness is just a verbal device that solves nothing. In Sartre's own idiosyncratic recasting, on the other hand, self-deception (which is one of the translations of his *mauvaise foi*) is an attempt to suppress our fundamentally human and anxiety-provoking freedom. One of his famous examples is the waiter who takes on his identity as a waiter so thoroughly as to reduce his whole being to nothing more than that role.

We do not need to entertain any fanciful inner entities to shed light on the ordinary phenomenon of self-deception. A way out of the paradox is to say that self-deception is not an exact parallel of inter-personal deception (Mele, 1987, 2001). The suggestion is that self-deception is an instance of *motivationally biased belief*, which means that our wanting something to be the case has a biasing influence on the acquisition and retention of a belief for which we have contrary evidence. But this process need not be intentional.

A self-deceived person is therefore someone who believes something that he or she would not have believed in the absence of a particular interest that he or she has in the matter. The self-deception lies not in the holding of two contradictory beliefs but in coming to believe something false as a result of a desire for a certain state of affairs to be true. While not exactly the same as wishful thinking – which is believing without adequate evidence rather than in the face of strong contrary evidence – the two phenomena are seen to lie on the same continuum. Both are kinds of motivationally biased thinking, in the sense that the desire for something to be the case has a biasing influence on our fact-finding. This can happen in a number of ways (Mele, 1987, 2001):

- *negative misinterpretation*: our desire that p leads us to misinterpret as not counting against p data that we would normally consider as counting against p;
- *positive misinterpretation*: our desire that p leads us to interpret as support for p evidence that we would normally recognise to count against p;
- *selective focusing/attending*: our desire that p leads us to fail to focus our attention on evidence that counts against p and to focus instead on evidence that supports it;
- *selective evidence-gathering*: our desire that p leads us both to over-look easily obtained evidence against p and to look for less accessible evidence in favour of p.

In all these the evidence is handled inappropriately as a result of desire. So our desire that p leads us to fail to appreciate the evidence against p, to misconstrue the relevance of this evidence, to fail to locate readily available evidence against p and to focus selectively on evidence in support of p.

Let us imagine that Nathan has a consuming desire to marry Alice. The evidence in his possession should suggest that she is unlikely to share the feeling, and that she is not even interested in anything other than a friendly relationship with him. But because he wants it so badly, his attention is captivated by what he perceives as evidence in favour of his eventual success (such as Alice seeming especially friendly towards him on a particular occasion), while deflecting all evidence against it (even if Alice is explicit about not wanting a romantic relationship with him, Nathan can explain it away by, for instance, convincing himself that Alice is going through a difficult time and does not know her own mind). If he carefully weighed up the facts he would probably arrive at the conclusion that this marriage is not on the cards but because he selectively pays attention only to evidence in favour of Alice's interest, he comes to a hopeful conclusion instead. Desire affects interest, and interest affects attention. Holding the false belief may also have the subjectively positive side-effect of reducing anxiety.

These mental processes are purposive in the sense that they serve a purpose within the self-deceiver's mental economy, but they are not *intentional*. The main distinction here is that these processes exist as a result of some purpose or interest that we have, but it is not the case that we initiate and direct them *because* we recognise that they serve some such interest.

Critical Thinking

Thinking clearly is a fundamental skill for making decisions. We need to cultivate the sound reasoning habits that will allow us to identify and avoid self-deception and to minimise the interference of fallacies and distortions. This is likely to be an uphill struggle, however: irrationality seems to be the order of the day in human beings, not only because of the turbulent influence of emotions and desires, but also as a result of the flaws inherent in the way we think. We know that we are subject to unmotivated ('cold') biased beliefs as well as motivationally biased ones (Mele, 2001). Some common sources of bias are:

- how vivid the information is;
- how accessible the information is;
- our tendency to search for confirming rather than disconfirming evidence;
- our tendency to look for causal explanations (which, as a result of the other sources of bias, is likely to lead us to form and retain ill-founded hypotheses).

How can these – and other – distortions be counteracted? According to Sutherland (1992), the methods include:

- keeping an open mind;
- surveying all evidence;
- seeking evidence that disconfirms our own beliefs;
- paying attention to any such evidence if we find it;
- looking for flaws in the arguments in favour of our own views;
- avoiding making decisions under stress;
- suspending judgement if the evidence is inconclusive.

Generally, in the fraught process of acquiring sound beliefs about the world, we could do with criteria to sort beliefs into those we want to accept, those we want to reject and those about which we want to suspend judgement. Certainty, alas, is not frequently achievable in life. Things cannot often be proved right or wrong beyond all doubt, and more often than not we have to be content with adopting the beliefs that are best supported by the available evidence. A few principles of what could be called 'mental hygiene' (Baggini, 2002b) may be helpful:

- We should avoid adopting inconsistent beliefs.
- If we reasonably believe a particular statement, we should also believe all the other statements that follow from it as a matter of logic.
- For most statements about the world, we should pursue probability rather than certainty.
- If a statement and its contradictory are equally probable, we should suspend judgement; otherwise we should adopt the more probable of the two.
- We should avoid believing statements just because they *may* be true, or have not been proved wrong. Instead, we should look for the balance of probability.
- We should regard our views as hypotheses to be tested rather than dogmas.
- In deciding between competing explanations, we should
  - prefer the one that fits in with well-established facts unless we have good reasons to do otherwise;
  - prefer the simpler over the more elaborate, other things being equal;
  - prefer the one that has greater explanatory power.

Selecting the Right Steps towards Our Goals

According to Aristotle, once people have decided on a goal, they:

> go on to think about how and by what means it is to be achieved. If it
> appears that there are several means available, they consider by which it
> will be achieved in the easiest and most noble way; while if it can be
> attained by only one means, they consider how this will bring it about,
> and by what further means this means is itself to be brought about.
>
> (*NE*, Book III, Ch. 3)

So once we have decided to train as a doctor, say, we need to think
about what steps are necessary to achieve our goal, such as what college
to go to or how to finance the course. We may need to take some
further steps before we are able to enrol on a course, such as fulfilling
entry criteria or saving some money. We also need to monitor whether
our plan is working, and to revise it if it proves unfruitful, or too costly
in some way: how easy or difficult is it to implement it? Is it leading to
the achievement of our goals? Is it having any unforeseen negative
consequences? Do we need to revise the goal or the plan? And so
on.

Finally, we may want to remember Russell's (1930/1975, p. 56)
advice:

> It is amazing how much both happiness and efficiency can be increased
> by the cultivation of an orderly mind, which thinks about a matter ade-
> quately at the right time rather than inadequately at all times. When a
> difficult or worrying decision has to be reached, as soon as all the data
> are available, give the matter your best thought and make your decision;
> having made the decision, do not revise it unless some new fact comes
> to your knowledge. Nothing is so exhausting as indecision, and nothing
> is so futile.

Once a decision has been made on the basis of our best knowledge and
understanding, we should strongly discourage any urges to revisit it
unless something significant has changed in the meantime.

INTUITION

There is a bias in many forms of counselling and psychotherapy towards
'going with the heart', doing what 'feels right' and following our intuition rather than relying on more analytic decision-making methods.

The fear seems to be that using these might turn us into calculating robots. But the value of intuition should not be accepted uncritically, and it should not be assumed that 'heart reasons' need always trump other kinds of reasons.

Intuition is big business. Intuition workshops offer potential participants all sorts of benefits arising from the awakening of their intuitive powers. A quick perusal of the Amazon booklist reveals titles such as:

Seven steps to developing your intuitive powers
Understanding and teaching the intuitive mind
Intuition: the path to inner wisdom
Developing intuition
Living intuitively
Intuitive way: a guide to living from inner wisdom

and even:

The complete idiot's guide to making money through intuition.

A trip to the local library reveals a similar array of titles. But what do we actually mean by 'intuition'?

According to the *Oxford Companion to Philosophy*, intuition is:

> an alleged direct relation, analogous to visual seeing, between the mind and something abstract and so not accessible to the senses. What are intuited (which can be derivatively called 'intuitions') may be abstract objects, like numbers or properties, or certain truths regarded as not accessible to investigation through the senses or calculation; the mere short-circuiting of such processes in 'bank manager's intuition' would not count as intuition for philosophy.
>
> (Honderich, 1995, p. 415)

This parallels the common view of intuition as something other than and alien from our ordinary reasoning faculties, a mysterious inner power that some people can invoke to get instant solutions to all sorts of problems. But intuition is not that reliable. A friend of mine confesses that every time he flies he has the 'intuition' that the plane will crash. That is the problem with this kind of intuition: we can never know whether to trust it or not, since, without realising it, we could be listening to deeply engrained fears and prejudices or unrealistic hopes rather than to the voice of our inner wisdom: is intuition really a 'capacity for direct knowledge, for immediate insight without observation or reason' or, rather more sceptically, an 'inner knowing that we're right, whether we are or not'? (Myers, 2004, p. 1).

Myers (2004) sets out to explore the powers and perils of intuition, and finds plenty of empirical evidence of both. It is widely accepted nowadays that we vastly overestimate the extent of our conscious control on everyday thinking, feeling and acting, and that much processing goes on 'behind the scenes', outside conscious awareness (this is very different from an unconscious of a Freudian variety). Our thinking, memory and attitudes seem to operate on two levels, one controlled (conscious, rational, analytic) and one automatic (simple, intuitive, non-verbal). Both of these are at work within us all the time.

On the positive side, this non-conscious processing enables us, for instance, to 'read' people's feelings and intentions, to infer their character traits and make predictions about them on the basis of mere fragments of their behaviour. The 'ability of our unconscious to find patterns in situations and behaviour based on very narrow slices of experience' has become known as 'thin-slicing' (Malcolm Gladwell, in *The Guardian*, 19/1/05, p. 7). According to Gladwell, '[w]hen we leap to a decision or have a hunch, our unconscious is . . . sifting through the situation in front of us, throwing out all that is irrelevant while we zero in on what really matters. And the truth is that our unconscious is really good at this, to the point where thin-slicing often delivers a better answer than more deliberate and exhaustive ways of thinking.'

Myers (2004) also reports that in some circumstances gut feelings are remarkably accurate. In one experiment, students were asked to rate thirteen teachers on a number of scales, such as confidence and warmth, on the basis of ten-second video clips of teaching. These ratings turned out accurately to predict further ratings taken at the end of the semester. Another striking feature that we display is the ability to interpret non-verbal clues across cultures. These embodied intuitive capacities are the result of a mixture of hard-wired systems, classical conditioning processes and our own particular emotional histories.

But, as Myers (2004) points out, there is a more menacing side to this. In another experiment, for instance, students were shown a videotape of a schoolgirl named Hannah taking a test in which she got some answers right and some wrong. Half the students had previously viewed Hannah videotaped in a depressed urban setting, while the other half had seen her videotaped in an affluent suburban area. The former went on to surmise low cognitive ability and recalled her getting most of the answers wrong; the latter inferred higher ability and remembered her getting most of the answers right. This shows that when we make judgements about other people, we are vulnerable to subtle distorting influences of which we may be unaware.

For all its usefulness, it would appear, intuitive information processing is also highly fallible. Our memories are to some degree constructed as we go along, and may be distorted. I have a clear and vivid recollection of a childhood television series featuring Roger Moore and Tony Curtis playing two detectives, in which the Roger Moore character had died but turned up as a ghost to help the Tony Curtis character with his investigations. But not so long ago I reluctantly had to accept that no such series ever existed: there were, instead, two separate programmes: *The Persuaders*, featuring RM and TC but no detectives whatsoever, and *Randall and Hopkirk Deceased*, with different actors, in which the plot did indeed revolve around a detective and his ghostly partner.

Continuing with this catalogue of woes, we seem to have a striking tendency to rewrite history and filter memories to suit our current views or moods. We are apt to make up reasons for our actions after the event, so there is a sense in which at times we don't know our minds or why we do what we do. We confabulate, and fill in the gaps, but if there are subtle influences at work 'our intuitions may be radically mistaken' (Myers, 2004, p. 78). We are not very good at predicting our own feelings, and we overestimate the extent to which we would be happy if we achieved desired outcomes or upset if unexpected misfortunes were to befall us. We often mispredict our own behaviour, and we are unrealistically optimistic about the future. We believe we always knew things that we know only in hindsight. We exaggerate our importance. We tend to attribute good outcomes to our own efforts and bad outcomes to external factors, but do the opposite in relation to others. We see ourselves as better than average, but if we make a mistake we convince ourselves that most people would do the same. We are overconfident about our ability to change. And so on.

The upshot of all this is that we should indeed heed our hunches and gut feelings (it may be that at some level we are detecting something important), but should also take them with a big pinch of salt (we might just be falling prey to some kind of cognitive distortion) and ensure that we test them against reality and think critically. While the danger of succumbing to errors and fallacies is always present, we are less susceptible to it if we aim to correct our intuitions by using tests and mental hygiene methods such as those highlighted in the section on critical thinking. Intuitions, gut feelings, hunches, all have a place in rational decision-making; but only as one element among others, to be weighed up and examined rather than accepted uncritically.

Thagard (2001) reviews the pros and cons of making decisions by intuition or calculation. Advantages of intuitive decision-making include:

- speed;
- taking into account what we really care about;
- leading directly to action.

Disadvantages of the intuitive method include:

- we may fail to consider other options;
- there is a real danger of acting on unexamined cravings and addictions;
- our decision may be based on inaccurate or irrelevant information.

There is, however, another possible understanding of intuition, which refers to the ability of the person of practical wisdom to grasp the most important features of a situation and act on them without too much heartache. With time and practice, we may eventually reach a point where we are able to 'see' what the right thing to do is in the circumstances with no explicit deliberation. We could choose to call this 'intuition', but it is an intuition that is based on an acutely developed rationality rather than a separate faculty in competition with it. It is to this second sense of 'intuition' that Nussbaum (1994) is referring when she writes that '[s]ituations must be grasped with an "eye" for all their complexities' (p. 68) and that 'practical wisdom . . . is the "eye" of the soul' (p. 71).

CHANCE EVENTS

Pondering about life (and referring to safe sex) Carrie in *Sex and the City* muses:

> odd how only when our physical life is at risk do we follow certain guide-lines to protect ourselves. But what about our emotional lives? Wouldn't it be nice if there was a little pamphlet to warn what unsafe behaviour might be, high-risk to ourselves or our relationships?

Sadly, there could be no such book. There can be few rules that apply in all situations: human beings are too different, and the variables too many. But what *is* possible is to reflect on the kinds of considerations that should guide us when making important decisions, and ensure that at those times we take the correct steps in reasoning. This will make it more likely that we act in the light of our best values and select the best means towards our ends. Good deliberation is not based on guesswork, says Aristotle, and neither is it just the achievement of the required results. It is a matter of correctness in our reasoning.

Sometimes things develop in odd ways, and even unpromising situations or decisions can have unforeseen positive consequences. Take the case of Joe Simpson, an experienced mountaineer who seemed to suffer extreme bad luck when he broke his leg and subsequently fell into a crevasse on Siula Grande, in Peru, in 1985. He survived, however, and turned bad luck to good use when he wrote a book about the experience, which became a bestseller (and later a film) and launched his writing career. But let us manipulate the details a little: let us imagine that Joe_2 is a beginner at mountaineering who foolishly decides to take on a challenge for which he is ill prepared. He might be lucky and, like Joe_1, survive and become a successful author, but he is more likely to die or suffer serious injury.

Good deliberation does not guarantee that we will achieve our goals, because life comes with no warranties. We could simply be exceptionally unlucky. Conversely, we could be exceptionally lucky while not practically wise. However, if reasoning does not necessarily lead to the desired outcomes, we cannot count on luck to deliver. According to Sutherland (1992, p. 6):

> in human affairs there is almost always an element of chance. But over a lifetime chance tends to even out, and if you want to achieve your ends to the greatest possible extent, you had better take the rational decision as often as you can even though on occasion a different decision would have led to a better result.

Furthermore, if we have learned the art of good deliberation we will be able to make the most of our situation and will at any rate be applying the rational abilities that make us what we are.

Larmore (1999) is concerned that going through that tedious weighing of options all the time might not leave room for acting passionately and spontaneously, and reminds us that it is important to remain open to life's surprises. We can never fully know in advance the character of our good, and 'our happiness includes not just the anticipated good we achieve, but also the unexpected good which happens to us' (p. 103). He concludes that the good life 'is the life lived with a sense of our dual nature as active and passive beings, bent on achieving the goals we espouse, but also liable to be surprised by forms of good we never anticipated' (p. 111). Life is 'richer in possibilities' than we think, and adopting too rigid a notion of a life plan could close our minds to the lessons we might otherwise learn. Larmore also points out that 'our lives would mean less if they did not contain moments of wonder and redirection, when we find that earlier choices have led to a happiness we never imagined, or when we see our existing purposes thrown into disarray by the realization that our fulfillment lies elsewhere' (p. 112).

But practical wisdom can accommodate all this. Spontaneity need not be hampered by the ability to resort to an explicit, rational decision-making process when the situation requires, since the situation does not always require it. It is only extreme spontaneity that could, just like extreme rationality, be detrimental to our well-being.

PRACTICAL APPLICATIONS

In *Out of Sheer Rage* (1997), Geoff Dyer gives a funny and insightful description of the perils of decision-making. The author – truthfully or otherwise – portrays himself as an appalling decision-maker, agonising about whether to move away from his apartment in Paris.

> I decided to sign a contract that would make me the official tenant . . . I wasn't even sure that I wanted to stay in an apartment where I had actually been extremely unhappy for ninety per cent of my stay, where ninety per cent of my stay had been dominated by anxiety about (a) whether I was going to stay and (b) whether I was going to start a novel or start my study of Lawrence, but as soon as the managing agents said that they were unwilling to let the place to me . . . I became convinced that I had to stay in this apartment where I had been sublimely happy, that there was, in fact, nowhere else on earth where I could hope to be as content.

The agents agree, and he signs the lease:

> I was ecstatic. For about five minutes. Then I realised I had taken on an awesome, not to say crippling responsibility . . . The one thing I could be

sure of was that I had to leave this apartment, where I had never known a moment's peace of mind, as soon as possible.

(pp. 7–8)

He renounces the flat, un-renounces it, renounces it again and tries to un-renounce it again, until the decision is taken out of his hands and he has to go.

Our own experiences may be less extreme, but many of us will be familiar with this exasperating decisional seesaw. Many people have trouble with making decisions in one way or another. Where do we go wrong? These are some of the possibilities:

1. We avoid decisions until they are looming, or until it is too late. We may achieve this, for instance, through:
   - wishful thinking (convincing ourselves that 'it will be OK');
   - prioritising short-term tasks;
   - diversionary activities (such as filling our life with other engagements);
   - trying to keep our options open;
   - holding out for the perfect solution.
2. We keep wavering between options, unable to make up our minds.
3. We come to a decision, but then immediately change our minds.

Both (2) and (3) may be due to some kind of shift in values. If we are looking for a place to live, for instance, the relative importance of two potentially conflicting values – such as living in a nice area and containing the costs – may appear different at different times, or before and after a decision. These and other difficulties could be at least to some degree counteracted by a sound decision-making process that includes an exploration of values.

Benjamin Franklin was once asked for advice on decision-making, and he gave the following answer (cited in Sutherland, 1992):

> I cannot, for want of sufficient premises, advise you *what* to determine, but if you please I will tell you *how*. . . . My way is to divide half a sheet of paper by a line into two columns; writing over one *Pro* and over the other *Con*. Then, during three or four days' consideration, I put down under the different heads short hints of the different motives, that at different times occur to me *for* or *against* the measure. When I have thus got them all together in one view, I endeavour to estimate the respective weights . . . [to] find at length where the balance lies. . . . And, though the weight of reasons cannot be taken with the precision of algebraic quanti-

ties, yet, when each is thus considered, separately and comparatively, and the whole matter lies before me, I think I can judge better, and am less liable to make a rash step; and in fact I have found great advantage for this kind of equation, in what may be called *moral* or *prudential algebra*.

(p. 272)

Thagard (2001) suggests combining both intuitive and 'calculative' decision-making methods by giving emotions, hunches and desires their due importance, while at the same time trying to avoid fallacies and biases due to flawed intuitions. He therefore advises us to:

- reflect carefully on the decision to be made;
- reflect on the different goals and their respective importance;
- reflect on the various options and the extent to which they are likely to facilitate the goal;
- consider the available evidence as well as emotional distortions or any other sources of bias.

But we may not be able to do this on our own: sometimes we look 'inside ourselves' and find only an opaque, murky chaos, and we are unable to tell good reasons from bad. In relation to this, Aristotle states that '[o]n important issues, we do not trust our own ability to decide and call in others to help us deliberate' (Book III, Ch. 3). In such cases counsellors and therapists could help clients to:

- think clearly about themselves and their situation;
- see through wishful thinking and self-deception;
- pinpoint irrational thinking;
- examine the reasons for and against particular courses of action;
- identify genuine values and reasons;
- ensure that all relevant considerations are included;
- assess whether particular emotions point to true value or are based on distortions;
- establish the balance of reasons;
- eliminate spurious reasons;
- reach an overall judgement based on a careful assessment of the situation;
- select the right means to their ends.[5]

---

[5]For a comprehensive decision-making method, see www.decision-making.co.uk.

Let us take the example[6] of Simone, a middle-aged woman, in precarious work and housing circumstances and in a new relationship, who is torn over whether to have an abortion. It would do no good at all to encourage her to do what she feels: *that* is how she feels, torn between different emotions and considerations. She should be helped to identify and examine her emotions, which may include hopes and worries about the likely positive or negative consequences of having a baby at this stage in her life and in her relationship: for instance, anxieties about being an older mother and about how she would cope as a single mother if the relationship ended, fantasies about the happy family life that has eluded her so far, fears that this might be her last chance to have a baby and that she might later regret it if she didn't go through with the pregnancy.

It would also be important to explore Simone's beliefs about relevant ethical issues such as the sanctity of life or women's right to self-determination. She should be helped to reflect on these – establishing how they fit in with each other, with other important beliefs that she may have, and with the likely consequences of her decision – and to identify assumptions and contradictions. This dialogue may yield an answer that is an obvious winner or it may not – perhaps the thoughts and emotions that pull her in different directions really are all relevant and appropriate, and the best she can do is to choose what, on the basis of her current information, she can reasonably conclude to be the lesser evil. According to Cohen and Cohen (1999), we need to draw a distinction between 'feeling good about what one has done and having done what was right in the given situation' (p. 37).

Simone may therefore decide that the right thing to do all things considered is to have the abortion; but this would not imply that her misgivings were therefore unfounded. Even if the decision reached is not clear-cut, however, she should still greatly benefit from having gone through this process – at least she would have come to understand her contrasting emotions better, subjected her beliefs to scrutiny, and carefully weighed the issues at stake, and could rest secure in the knowledge that she had taken the issue very seriously. Her decision, while not necessarily comfortable, would at least be reasoned and based on her best possible judgement at the time.

There is a great danger that counsellors and psychotherapists may exert a subtle influence on clients who are struggling to make a

---

[6]A version of this has previously appeared in an article entitled 'Moral dilemmas and the counsellor', *Counselling and Psychotherapy Journal*, 14, 8 (2003).

decision: as a result of their own biases, therapists may affect clients' deliberations just by drawing attention to some aspects of a situation rather than others, asking certain questions rather than others, or even nodding in some places rather than others. It is particularly important, therefore, to turn the therapy process into a joint investigation into the best reasons for action.

3

The Virtues of Character: Feeling the Fear and Doing It Anyway?

Not many of us spend sleepless nights worrying about becoming more virtuous or are likely to consult a therapist to do this – but perhaps all this tells us is that the word 'virtue' can be misleading. According to Williams (1985, p. 9): 'The word "virtue" has for the most part acquired comic or otherwise undesirable associations, and few now use it except philosophers, but there is no other word that serves as well, and it has to be used in moral philosophy.'

In fact clients often bring to therapy issues related to the ancient understanding of virtue: they may want to be more able to take risks, be more patient, more confident, more autonomous, more tenacious, more assertive, kinder to their spouse or family, less inclined to give in to temptations and immediate gratifications. They may wonder whether they are pushing themselves too hard or not hard enough, at what point tolerance gives way to being a doormat or courage to recklessness, or what the right balance is between achievement and enjoyment. All this criss-crosses the ancient territory of virtue.

While many people seek a counsellor or therapist to resolve some immediate problem, implicitly or explicitly there is often a dissatisfaction, a gap between the kind of person they are and the kind of person they would like to be: they do or feel something too much or too often, or too little or not often enough, and they want to change this. Underlying the question 'What shall I do now?' are often other questions: 'What kind of person do I want to be? Which aspects of myself do I need to develop, and which to curb or correct?' These questions may be used as tests in particular decisions ('What kind of person would I be if I did this or that?') but also form the core of a more general kind of reflection, which most of us entertain at some point in our life. Whether we realise it or not, these concerns are likely to enter the therapy process, and it can be useful to engage with them directly, with the aim of helping clients in their project of self-formation, of developing the best character they can.

THE VIRTUES OF CHARACTER

If we were told that in order to have a good life we needed to become virtuous, we would probably visualise a somewhat pious existence in which we give to the poor or refrain from any naughty doings. The word 'virtue' is to blame here, directing our attention to the narrowest kind of moral judgement and hinting at an ability to resist carnal temptations. But the Greek word *aretê* preceded the moral distinctions that through Christianity have come to be embodied in the word 'virtue', and these connotations were absent from it. An alternative translation of *aretê* is 'excellence', which however has misleading connotations of its own (see footnote, p. xv). Bearing this in mind, it is best to delve into the concept to try to understand how it worked in ancient ethics and how it might help us now.

According to Aristotle, the virtues are the main ingredient of the flourishing life. If we go back to *eudaimonia* we will remember that, as well as a certain amount of good fortune, having a good life requires developing our distinctive human capacities to the best of our ability. This involves developing reason and the virtues. Aristotle divided the virtues into two types: *intellectual virtues* and *virtues of character.* Intellectual virtues are a direct expression of reason, and include theoretical and practical reason (or wisdom). Here I will concentrate on the virtues of character, which are merely *responsive* to reason. Aristotle's explanation of the concept begins with the idea of something 'being excellent of its kind'. Let us see how this works when applied to things other than human beings.

Eyes:
The virtue of the eye, for example, makes it and its characteristic activity good, because it is through the virtue of the eye that we see well.
(*NE*, Book II, Ch. 6)

Horses (an anthropocentric view):
Likewise, the virtue of the horse makes a horse good – good at running, at carrying its rider and at facing the enemy.
(*NE*, Book II, Ch. 6)

In relation to us, Aristotle begins by saying that 'the virtue of a human being too will be the state that makes a human being good and makes him perform his characteristic activity well' (*NE*, Book II, Ch. 6). There is a way of being that is the human equivalent of a horse's being good at running, at carrying its rider and at facing the enemy: but what is it? Undeniably, certain areas of life are problematic for us, and can get in the way of living well. In order to have a good life we need to become skilled at handling the spheres of life and action that are most challenging for us and in which it is easiest to 'get it wrong'. These have to do with emotions, desires, and generally pleasure and pain. Getting it right in these areas means that our judgements, feelings and actions are in harmony and are appropriate to the circumstances. This is important both in itself, in that it is a way of living according to reason, and for the attainment of other valuable goals.

Being virtuous is therefore a step beyond simply arriving at the right judgement in decision-making or performing the right action. It means that our feelings, desires and intentions are in tune with our reason. We tend to have conflicting intuitions about this. Is it more virtuous to struggle against competing motivations and win, or to do the right thing effortlessly, with our judgement and feelings in harmony? Although there is a certain heroic appeal about the former, the latter seems a more desirable state of affairs. For Aristotle, if we end up doing the right thing after struggling against competing motivation, we will have exhibited self-control. Virtue, on the other hand, is displayed only when reason and feelings are in line. The person who manages to overcome strong feelings may indeed be admirable, but would not be virtuous. In relation to this, Annas (1993, p. 54) writes that 'We can admire someone overcoming a handicap without thinking it preferable to have that handicap'.

The virtues are often seen as corrective in situations where there is a temptation to be resisted or a deficiency of motivation to be made up for (Foot, 1978). If this means that the virtues actually help us to counter unhelpful desires and motives in particular situations, it is the wrong characterisation of virtue: the virtuous person does not normally have to fight down countering feelings and motivations, since conquering these belongs to the sphere of self-control. The virtues are corrective, however, in the sense that they come into play in areas of life in which such feelings and motivations are often present for many of us. As Foot points out, the reason why courage and temperance are virtues is that fear and desire for pleasure exist and do not always lead us in the right direction (so we may want to run away or seek pleasure at times when we should not). Similar considerations apply to other virtues. If we were constituted differently, there would be no need for this kind of correction.

The virtues are stable dispositions to grasp the right thing to do and do it gladly, to act and feel in accordance with reason. Clearly, in each given situation we have a limited amount of control over this: it is not always possible to summon up the right feelings at the right time. Acquiring a virtue, therefore, is a long-term project rather than an instant achievement. We cannot become courageous or generous overnight. Perhaps we can push ourselves to *act* courageously or generously; but, as we have seen, that is not what being virtuous is about. We are still responsible for our character, however, for if we realise that it is important for us to develop certain virtues, we can take steps that will eventually enable us to do the right thing with ease. This means encouraging in ourselves the tendency to *want* to follow the dictates of reason and cultivating the traits, attitudes and habits that help us to have balanced responses to situations.

THE VIRTUES OF CHARACTER AND PRACTICAL WISDOM

The virtues of character are closely connected to practical wisdom, which is the disposition to make the right judgements. The person who has practical wisdom has learned the right way of reasoning, especially regarding moral matters, and is able to apply it consistently. The virtues of character are attitudes and feelings that complement the right judgements. In any given situation, the right thing to do is determined by reason in decision-making, and the virtues enable us to follow this judgement without struggle. The relationship is reciprocal, however, since the more virtuous we are the easier it will be to make the right decisions. According to Annas (1993), the right judgements both presuppose and develop the tendency to have the appropriate feelings.

There seems to be something of a mismatch between the idea of, perhaps laboriously, weighing things up in order to come up with a judgement about what to do and the effortless actions of the virtuous person. One way to resolve this tension is by saying that deliberation does not have to refer to a psychological process, but can also refer to the 'structure of reasoned explanation' (Broadie, 1991, p. 79). While the person who is developing the virtues is likely to go through an explicit process of weighing up options, the fully virtuous person will be able, in most instances, simply to apprehend certain aspects of a situation as being salient and providing reasons for action in such a way as to silence other reasons (McDowell, 2003). This is clearly an ideal that few people will reach, however, and it is likely that even the virtuous person will have to engage in a certain amount of problem-solving for reasons unrelated to lack of virtue (Annas, 1993).

To what extent do we need to have virtue considerations at the front of our minds when reasoning about what to do in particular situations? Williams (1985) raises the point that there may be something 'suspect' about choosing particular actions *because* they are the generous or brave thing to do – almost as if we were looking at ourselves through the lens of what other people would say about us and what we do. Someone with a virtue will tend to choose particular actions because they are the right thing to do in terms of the available reasons, not because they exemplify a virtue: 'a courageous person does not typically choose acts as being courageous, and . . . [t]he benevolent or kindhearted person does benevolent things, but does them under other descriptions, such as "she needs it," "it will cheer him up," "it will stop the pain"' (p. 10). We need to train ourselves to want to act on the right reasons.

On the other hand, as Williams recognises, developing our character will involve a certain amount of reflection on what our actions and feelings betray about us and our values. This may at times feature in our decision-making: if we have realised that we should become more generous, for instance, we will need to ask ourselves whether the actions we have performed or are contemplating are in tune with the kind of person we want to be.

THE DOCTRINE OF THE MEAN

But we need to know more about how to characterise the virtues. Aristotle says that:

> For example, fear, confidence, appetite, anger, pity, and in general pleasure and pain can be experienced too much or too little, and in both ways not well. But to have them at the right time, about the right things, towards the right people, for the right end, and in the right way, is the mean and best; and this is the business of virtue. Similarly, there is an excess, a deficiency and a mean in actions.
>
> (*NE*, Book II, Ch. 6)

The virtuous person aims for 'the mean' in feelings and actions and avoids excess and deficiency, which are two opposite ways of getting things wrong. An important point that Aristotle makes is that the mean he is talking about is *relative* to people and situations rather than absolute, as in the case of the arithmetic mean. He makes this point so well that it would be a pity not to read it in his words:

> If, for example, ten are many and two are few, six is the mean if one takes it in respect of the thing, because it is by the same amount that it exceeds the one number and is exceeded by the other. This is the mean according to arithmetic progression. The mean relative to us, however, is not to be obtained in this way. For if ten pounds of food is a lot for someone to eat, and two pounds a little, the trainer will not necessarily prescribe six; for this may be a lot or a little for the person about to eat it – for Milo, [a famous athlete] a little, for a beginner at gymnastics, a lot. The same goes for running and wrestling.
>
> (*NE*, Book II, Ch. 6)

The mean is often mistaken for moderation, and as a result this theory has been accused of being bland and uninteresting. But the mean is not undifferentiated moderation. If we take the example of anger, we will see that it hardly makes sense to say that we should always have a moderate amount of anger, since most situations require no anger at all and some situations require great anger. Urmson (1980, p. 161) writes that 'The man whose character is such that he feels only mild annoyance at a trivial slight and is enraged by torture has a character that is in a mean between one that exhibits rage on trivial as well as important occasions and one that can coolly contemplate the greatest outrages'. In order to develop the virtues it is important to learn to discriminate between situations and to train ourselves to act according to what they require of us. We could, for instance, cultivate the habit of not getting angry at the wrong people or for unimportant things.

The excess–deficiency model does not always apply, says Aristotle, and some things are just bad, such as 'spite, shamelessness, envy, and, among actions, adultery, theft, homicide'. In these cases, it is not possible to hit the mark – 'committing adultery, say, with the right woman, at the right time, or in the right way' (*NE*, Book II, Ch. 6) – and one always misses.

At what point does foolhardiness turn into courage and courage into timidity? It must be a continuum rather than discrete states. It could be argued that if we cannot determine the cut-off point between mean and extremes the distinction is useless. This objection may be illustrated through a well-known paradox. You have a heap of sand. You take away one grain. Then another. Then another, until you have no sand left. But at what point did the heap cease to be a heap? Surely removing just one grain can never make the difference between having a heap and having no heap. This is an instance of a notorious philosophical puzzle (the problem of vagueness) that, thankfully, does not belong here. But clearly we can meaningfully talk about heaps even in the absence of a clear cut-off point. The same applies to the mean: the fluidity of the concept does not invalidate the usefulness of the distinction.

TRAINING OURSELVES TO CHANGE

The ideal to aim for is therefore that of a balanced character, with motivation in line with rational judgement and the right actions flowing effortlessly. But this does not happen overnight, and in order to develop such a harmonious character we need to train ourselves over a period of time. While the inclination to act in accordance with reason does not occur naturally and needs to be built up, our capacity to change the way we feel and behave *is* innate. In this respect we are unlike the many entities that obey only the laws of physics and cannot be made to behave differently from what their nature dictates. Our main tool to effect this kind of character training is what Aristotle calls *habituation*:

> For example, a stone that naturally falls downwards could not be made by habituation to rise upwards, not even if one tried to habituate it by throwing it up ten thousand times; nor can fire be habituated to burn downwards, nor anything else that naturally behaves in one way be habituated to behave differently. So virtues arise in us neither by nature nor contrary to nature, but nature gives us the capacity to acquire them, and completion comes through habituation.
>
> (*NE*, Book II, Ch. 1)

While the intellectual virtues are learned through teaching, training ourselves to acquire new qualities, skills and attitudes is achieved mainly by exercising them: 'for example, we become builders by building, and lyre-players by playing the lyre. So too we become just by doing just actions, temperate by temperate actions, and courageous by courageous actions' (*NE*, Book II, Ch. 1). On the nature–nurture continuum, Aristotle clearly leans towards nurture. It is possible to change the way we are simply by, in the first instance, acting differently.

Another relevant continuum is the relative importance of childhood upbringing and later learning. Aristotle gives great importance to upbringing, to the extent of saying that it makes 'all the difference' (*NE*, Book II, Ch. 1). This might give us the impression that if our early training had been lacking we would have slim hopes of changing and developing our characters. We might feel justified in blaming our parents or early environment for all our flaws, and give up on any attempt at self-improvement. But Aristotle would strongly disapprove of that. He says explicitly that people are responsible for their character – 'responsible for being unjust by doing wrong, or intemperate by spending their time in drinking and the like; in each sphere people's activities give them the corresponding character' (*NE*, Book III, Ch. 5). Even if our genes and our early training have not given us the best start in life, we still have the choice to stagnate or to move forward, to blame our past or to develop our talents to the extent that we can.

Over time, the accumulated effect of our choices will lead to the establishment of new habits of acting and feeling. Eventually, self-control and vigilant choice should give way to established inclinations and dispositions. Annas (1993) recognises that the introduction of habit into this picture could give the impression that acting out of virtue is akin to acting unthinkingly or mechanically. But she points out that this could never be the case, since the virtues are 'built up from repeated choices and the development of habits of choice' (p. 51) and on each occasion involve making a choice.

Aristotle realises that hitting the mean – perceiving the right thing to do and doing it gladly – is not always easy, and that sometimes we are just not sure what to do. His advice is that in such situations we should choose the lesser evil. He offers two rules of thumb:

- steer away from the more harmful extreme;
- steer away from the extreme towards which you are naturally inclined.

So we should train ourselves to act in ways that appear, for instance, mildly extravagant if we know that we usually tend towards stinginess, a little risky if we are normally timid, and so on for all the virtues.

An interesting analogy for this comes from a technique employed in navigation and known as 'aiming off':

Let us say you are walking across country and are aiming for a particular point on a stream. If you go straight for it and luck is on your side you may find the point first time. The likelihood is that you will hit the stream either upstream or downstream of the point. The question is, which? If you deliberately aim off slightly to one side you will know which way to turn when you get to the stream. The technique can be applied to any linear feature, a footpath, a ridge, a wall, etc.

(Langmuir, 1993, p. 43)

THE VIRTUES AND POSITIVE PSYCHOLOGY

Many definitive lists of virtues have been produced through history. One of the latest is the one put forward by the Positive Psychology movement, which is promoting a 'rehabilitation' of the virtues, albeit recast in a mould shaped by the discipline of psychology. After scouring the world's religious and philosophical traditions, Peterson and Seligman (2004) proposed a classification according to which there are six main universal virtues: wisdom and knowledge; courage; humanity; justice; temperance; and transcendence. These, however, were considered too abstract and general to be suitable for empirical investigation, and as a result the authors decided to concentrate their efforts on what they call 'character strengths': supposedly more concrete, but equally universal, processes and mechanisms that underlie the virtues. This is the structure they came up with:

Virtue	*Character strengths*
Wisdom and knowledge	Creativity, curiosity, open-mindedness, love of learning, perspective
Courage	Bravery, persistence, integrity, vitality
Humanity	Love, kindness, social intelligence
Justice	Citizenship, fairness, leadership
Temperance	Forgiveness and mercy, humility, prudence, self-regulation
Transcendence	Appreciation of beauty and excellence, gratitude, hope, humour, spirituality

Like Aristotle before them, Peterson and Seligman are careful to point out that accuracy is not on the agenda in this sphere. They believe, however, that a comprehensive charting of the territory will help to develop assessment tools and eventually interventions to increase particular strengths of character and general well-being. They effectively address the possible (indeed, frequent) objection that there are no universally valued strengths and virtues by asking us to imagine a culture that did not believe in cultivating 'courage, honesty, perseverance, hope or kindness', and in which parents are not bothered by the prospect of their children growing up to be 'cowardly, dishonest, easily discouraged, pessimistic, and cruel' (p. 33).

While the authors account for their methods in some detail, the resulting divisions between virtues and strengths seem somewhat artificial: some of the strengths could be virtues in their own right, and others sit uneasily 'under' a particular virtue. But the main question is whether the whole enterprise can really enhance our pursuit of wisdom. Although the effort seems worthwhile and in some respects in tune with Aristotle's ethos, the language and techniques of empirical psychology seem at odds with the ethos of searching for wisdom.

The idea is that each of us has a small number of defining qualities, or 'signature strengths' – the ones 'that a person owns, celebrates, and frequently exercises' (p. 18) – and that by developing these we can come to live a more meaningful life. A questionnaire designed to identify our signature strengths is available (Seligman, 2003; www.authentichappiness.org). For each strength, we are presented with two statements, such as 'I control my emotions', or 'I avoid activities that are physically dangerous', and we are asked to rate each statement on a 1–5 scale of 'very much like me' to 'not at all like me'. The value of this procedure is that the resulting profile, though rough and ready, can direct us towards areas of our life that we would be well advised not to neglect.

But it is hard to avoid the feeling that this is no way to delve into a person's world-view and values. Questionnaires seem too crude a method to form part of a serious quest for self-understanding and development. Like most questionnaires, this one requires categorical rather than context-sensitive answers, and therefore is likely to issue cartoon-like results, devoid of nuance. It also gives us no clue as to whether the attitudes specified in each statement are virtuous or problematic: 'I control my emotions' could be either, as could 'I avoid activities that are physically dangerous' and many others. It is only in dialogue that the role of these attitudes and behaviours in our own mental ecology may be established and evaluated.

WHICH VIRTUES?

The most important traditional Greek virtues were courage, temperance, justice and wisdom. Later Christian philosophers added hope, faith and charity. Aristotle had his own list, which to some extent reflects the values of an upper-class Greek citizen of his time. Thus he included greatness of soul and magnificence, which probably do not strike us as the foremost qualities that we might need to work on in order to improve our character. Others, such as courage, even temper and generosity, are just as important now as they were in ancient Greece, although even these might turn out to have a somewhat different slant for us: if we said we wanted to become more courageous, for instance, we would be unlikely to mean that we ought to have more equanimity in facing death on the battlefield.[7]

On the other hand – as Positive Psychology reminds us – when we move away from culture-specific quirks, there is a great deal of overlap between cultures as regards what traits and attitudes are regarded as virtues. This is because there are areas of challenge in life that most people are likely to experience simply as a result of being human. In these spheres, striving for the elusive mean is both difficult and particularly important.

If we start thinking about it, we begin to notice the principle of excess and deficiency at work all around us: for instance, we can be people pleasing, submissive doormats or aggressive, rude and intolerant; stiflingly attached to our routines or compulsively in need of change; gullible and naïve or suspicious and cynical; flatterers or blunt; shy or forward; slaves to others' opinions or rebellious; stingy or wasteful; self-denying or selfish; self-deprecating or boastful; insecure or overconfident; fearful or reckless; sloppy or fastidious; apathetic or overactive; irresolute, indecisive and hesitant or stubborn and dogmatic; navel gazing or superficial; gloomy or prone to wishful thinking; austere or self-indulgent; impulsive or calculating; humourless or flippant; and so on. These examples – while nothing but approximations –

---

[7]Aristotle's list is as follows (*NE*, 2000, p. xviii):

Virtue	Sphere
Courage	Fear and confidence
Temperance	Bodily pleasure and pain
Generosity	Giving and retaining money
Magnificence	Giving and retaining money on a large scale
Greatness of soul	Honour on a large scale
[Nameless]	Honour on a small scale
Even temper	Anger
Friendliness	Social relations
Truthfulness	Honesty about oneself
Wit	Conversation
Justice	Distribution
Friendship	Personal relations

give a flavour of the kinds of issues that we might find ourselves or our clients grappling with.

There are undoubtedly many possible permutations of similar and other pairs. A comprehensive and definitive list seems out of our reach: the traits and attitudes that we may need to develop in order to have a good character and live a good life are probably too many to categorise neatly. However, the following are some particularly important areas in which the exercise of the virtues is likely to be called for:

1. Fear.
2. Enjoyment of sensual pleasures.
3. Anger.
4. Giving.

FEAR

Virtue: courage. Deficiency: timidity. Excess: foolhardiness.

Courage is clearly about handling fear, which arises from our perception of harm in the world. While Aristotle saw courage as primarily relating to valour in battle, we are likely to have a much more general understanding of the concept. Our aim in this sphere should be to feel fear appropriately. According to Aristotle, 'the courageous person is the one who endures and fears ... the right things, for the right reason, in the right way, and at the right time; for the courageous person feels and acts in accordance with the merits of the case, and as reason requires' (*NE*, Book III, Ch. 7). In practice this involves having a good grasp of what constitutes a threat and therefore should warrant fear.

What are people frightened of? Death, ill-health and disability, poverty, loss of loved ones and natural disasters must be near the top of the list. These are deeply rooted existential terrors that it is hard to eradicate from our lives. The Stoics argued that these things are not to be feared, and their point of view is discussed in the next chapter. Then there are scores of other fears: spiders, heights, the dark, open spaces, closed spaces, flying, public speaking, loneliness, rejection, failure, success, talking to strangers, making fools of ourselves, commitment and so on, down to the most bizarre, such as the fear of opening bank statements (this has apparently been identified as a phobia in its own right, said to affect millions of people). These may well be unrealistic or exaggerated; but they are still apt to have a debilitating impact on our lives, at which point they may be classified as phobias.

There can be a big discrepancy between the objective presence of danger and our subjective perception of risk or feelings of fear. Our fear may be alerting us to a real threat out there or it may be an ungrounded or at least wildly inflated assessment. The distinction between the two can get hopelessly blurred from a subjective point of view, which is why fear can be so ambiguous and hard to interpret. In order to develop the virtue of courage, we need to train ourselves to distinguish between appropriate and inappropriate fear responses.

I can think of several personal examples of not knowing how to 'read' my feelings of fear. One of them occurred on a walking trip to the Lake District some years ago. I dislike hill fog as much as I like hill walking, and on this occasion I was half-way up a mountain when a few wisps turned into all-enveloping fog, as a result of which I found myself quickly heading downhill. At the same time I could hear in the distance a small party with a dog carrying on up the mountain, chatting and seemingly unconcerned. Was it my fear that was inappropriate or their apparent lack of fear? Was I timid, or they foolhardy? What was the appropriate response to this situation? Of course we need to bear in mind the different circumstances: I was on my own, they were in a group; perhaps their navigation skills in low visibility conditions were better than mine; perhaps they knew the route well, I didn't; or they may have known something about the weather forecast that I didn't know. Our means, the appropriate feelings and actions, might have been very different.

Some cases are clearer: it would be no great show of courage to attempt to climb Everest wearing canvas shoes and having failed to train for it (although early Alpine climbers came close to this). It would be foolhardy, and inappropriate not to feel fear about it. And usually it takes no courage at all to go and get a pint of milk from the corner shop, so the person who fears it shows a deficiency of courage. But this is not necessarily the case: walking down the road could require courage if we lived in a very unsafe neighbourhood, for instance, or if we had been housebound due to injury or illness and were going out for the first time, or if we had reason to believe that snipers were lurking.

There are cases in which it might take courage to do things that most people do easily and without a second thought: for someone who has been suffering from agoraphobia and has long avoided leaving the house, getting on a bus may be a major achievement, requiring all the courage that he or she can muster. Sufferers may well know that they do not face any objective danger. But realising that something is not to be feared does not necessarily connect with our feelings, and therefore can represent only a first step towards virtue. By pushing ourselves to align at least our actions with our reason, a process of habituation should occur and our feelings should eventually follow. We must remember that the person who succeeds in conquering fear is admirable but not virtuous, although that process may lead to virtue.

Many people resort to self-help books to provide the answers, and the classic *Feel the Fear and Do it Anyway* (Jeffers, 1978) has been one of the most successful. There are some good points in it, such as that if we truly believed in our ability to handle anything that comes our way there would be little that could frighten us, or that a certain amount of fear is inevitable if we are expanding our comfort zone, and that the only way to conquer fear on any particular occasion is to go out and do it. It is not fear that is the problem, it is how we relate to it: 'We can't escape fear. We can only transform it into a companion that accompanies us in all our exciting adventures; it is not an anchor holding us transfixed in one spot' (p. 29). In order to change our attitude towards fear we need to train ourselves to control our perceptions and responses, so that we can start taking bigger risks.

We are warned that this does not apply to things that are physically dangerous or infringe on other people's rights, such as taking drugs, having an affair or robbing a bank, since these are unlikely in the long run to increase our ability to handle fear. But the tone of the book gives the impression that everything else is up for grabs. The problem with applying this to ourselves is that it can be very difficult to know when it is best to push ourselves to conquer our fear and when we should instead listen to it and withdraw. There is a tension between allowing fear to rule our life, and therefore stagnating within the perimeter of what we know, and taking on challenges that we are not ready for, thereby creating a life of constant stress and anxiety. The mean – pushing ourselves to a degree appropriate to the circumstances – can be hard to identify, and will depend on an accurate assessment of both objective danger (which in some situations can be difficult to make) and our ability to deal with our feelings. No self-help book can give us this answer, and it is not helpful to adopt blanket rules – for instance, to the effect that pushing ourselves is always or never good.

These are issues that clients frequently wish to address in therapy, and how we deal with them matters. Depending on the therapist's beliefs and attitudes, it would be easy to steer clients unwittingly towards one unhelpful extreme or another: they should be kind to

themselves, not push themselves too hard; or they should push themselves to take risks. Instead, we need to engage with the question and
help clients to identify the right risk to be taken at the right time and
in the right way. In order to decide whether or not to do it anyway they
will have to assess the importance of the goal, the objective danger,
how much risk they are prepared to take, whether they have or can
acquire the skills they need, how much stress and anxiety it would
cause them, whether it would conflict with other important aims they
have, who else is involved and how they might be affected, and so on.

What about that most fundamental of all fears, the fear of death? Is
there such a thing as a mean in this respect? Perhaps we could say that
to fear death appropriately might mean reminding ourselves that our
time here is limited and that we should not squander it, in the spirit in
which the Benedictine monks are exhorted to remind themselves daily
that they are going to die. Excessive fear of death may paralyse us, and
a lack of fear of death may push us to reckless action.

There are two main assessments that we have to make in relation to
fear: whether we typically tend to feel too much or too little fear; and
whether a particular fear is rational or irrational. Having arrived at a
judgement, we need to train ourselves to act accordingly, developing
our ability to follow that judgement as harmoniously as possible. Our
aim is to be able to recognise whether fear is warranted and let our
feelings and actions flow from that. Pushing ourselves to act despite
our irrational fears is admirable and important if it is done in the right
way. But although we may need to go through a phase in which we feel
the fear and do it anyway, it is far more important, according to
Aristotle, to come to *feel* in a way that is commensurate with the actual
danger we face.

ENJOYMENT OF SENSUAL PLEASURES

Virtue: temperance. Deficiency: insensitivity to pleasure. Excess:
overindulgence.

According to Aristotle, temperance and intemperance apply only to
the pleasures of the body, not those of the mind. But even among the
bodily pleasures, he makes a distinction between touch and taste on
the one hand and other senses on the other, saying that moderation is
required only in relation to the former. Other pleasures based on the
senses – such as looking at beautiful scenery, listening to music, appre-
ciating pleasant smells – are of a different nature. In her introduction

to the *Nicomachean Ethics* (2002) Broadie expands on this by saying that the pleasures of eating, drinking and sex are 'peculiarly "bodily"', and therefore the object of moderation, because 'what is enjoyed is sensations occurring in the organs as they operate in these functions'. This is contrasted with 'seeing and hearing, where we are equally dependent on bodily organs, but where the associated pleasures feature beautiful external objects, not one's own eyes and ears' (p. 26).

But Aristotle boils things down even more, and concludes that in fact it is only touch that needs to be handled with care:

> For the job of taste is to discriminate flavours, as do wine-tasters, or cooks preparing dishes; but people do not really enjoy these sorts of things – at least, intemperate people do not – but rather the gratification itself, which arises entirely through touch in the cases of food, drink and what people call the sexual pleasures.
>
> (*NE*, Book III, Ch. 10)

This is not a universal rule, however, and certain pleasures of touch, 'such as those produced in the gymnasium through massage and heat' (*NE*, Book III, Ch. 10), are also of a different nature, since it is not the body as a whole that is the province of the intemperate person, but only some parts of it.

This is a difficult area of life in which to get it right. We are constantly exposed to conflicting messages, which could be polarised as follows:

1. You are what you consume, therefore eat, drink, have sex, enjoy; buy now, pay later.
2. The joys of the flesh are empty and superficial and are guaranteed not to give lasting satisfaction, therefore you should look for meaning and value elsewhere.

The following Zen verse is intended to jolt us, through an unusual juxtaposition of images, into grasping the impermanence of body-related pursuits:

> A woman dressed up
> Over her skeleton:
> You call her
> An elegant lady?
> How funny!
>
> (Shigematsu, 1988, p. 36)

Which is right? We could make very different life choices, depending on whether we draw our values from, say, *Marie Claire* or Marcus Aurelius, so it is important to give the matter some thought. Could both be right, or at least have a substantial element of truth in them? If it is the case that every facet of human experience is to be valued, then although we should give more value to the activities that are distinctly human, such as those involving reason, we are by no means thereby required to shun the pleasures that come with our bodies.

The pleasures of the flesh do not give lasting satisfaction. And devoting all or most of our time and energy to the pursuit of immediate sensual gratification can prevent us from becoming involved in more valuable things and developing ourselves in more substantial ways. On the other hand, it is also true that a life totally devoid of sensual pleasure can be a limited and joyless life. An illustration of this can be found in the delightful film *Babette's Feast*, in which the dour inhabitants of an isolated community in Jutland thaw and mellow on eating the forbidden delights produced by the Parisian chef Babette, despite their previous pledge to protect themselves from sin by acting as if they had never tasted them. We are animals as much as we are rational, and barring all animal pleasures is likely to make for a sad, one-sided experience of life.

A balanced attitude towards the pleasures of the body might allow us to have the best of both worlds. Montaigne (1958) points out that such an attitude is likely to enhance pleasure rather than detracting from it: it is essential to approach sensual pleasures with moderation, 'for fear that, through lack of discretion, they may become mingled with pain. Excess is the bane of pleasure, and temperance is not its scourge but its seasoning' (p. 400). In more modern terms, Seligman (2003, p. 103) writes that bodily pleasures 'fade very rapidly once the external stimulus disappears, and we become accustomed to them very readily . . . , often requiring bigger doses to deliver the same kick as originally'; it is best, therefore, to spread out and savour our pleasures rather than go for the quantity approach.

In Aristotle's words, the intemperate person 'has an appetite for all pleasant things, or the most pleasant, and is led by his appetite to choose them *at the cost of everything else*' (my italics), while the person who is indifferent to all pleasures 'must be far from being human'. The person who hits the mean, on the other hand, enjoys sensual pleasures 'as long as they are not incompatible with health or vigour, contrary to what is noble, or beyond his means' (*NE,* Book III, Ch. 2). The mean in this sphere is about enjoying these things without making them the centre of our life, becoming unduly attached to them, or pursuing them to the extent that more valuable things suffer. The fuzzy area between healthy enjoyment and problematic dependence is an area that clients often struggle with and seek to clarify. This touches on the territory of 'addiction', which is addressed in Chapter Five.

ANGER

Virtue: even temper. Deficiency: placidity. Excess: bad temper.

One of Aristotle's most famous quotations is that we should aim to be angry 'at the right things and with the right people, as well as in the right way, at the right time, and for the right length of time' (*NE*, Book IV, Ch. 5). This means working out in practice when anger is appropriate and when it is not.

We are not so comfortable with the idea of emotions being appropriate or inappropriate. We have become used to thinking of emotions as just being there. And of course they are, but we tend to think of them as just there and *beyond assessment*. This seems especially true of anger. We worry about 'bottling anger in' and having to 'let it out', as if it were some mysterious fluid that, if prevented from escaping, would literally lead to the kinds of problems that may accrue as a result of pressure accumulating in a pressure cooker. But since we are not pressure cookers, this vivid metaphor is less than enlightening. Anger has less to do with pressure building up than with a way of thinking, an outlook, a judgement that we have been wronged – which of course can be assessed as appropriate or inappropriate.

Let us consider the following vignettes:

1. You are trying to park your car in a notoriously busy area. While you waste time trying to get into a place that is too small, a space becomes free a couple of cars away and is immediately taken by another passing car. You are furious.
2. You have had a bad day at work, where you got involved in a serious argument with your boss. When you go home you become very angry and shout at your daughter for misplacing the remote control.

Perhaps most people would agree that these are examples of inappropriate anger: the first because it is out of proportion and you have not been intentionally wronged, the second because it is out of proportion and directed at the wrong person. But there are many cases in which we would not be so sure. Would we be appropriately angry if our partner left us? What if our partner of ten years left us by fax, as has happened to a colleague of mine? Appropriate anger is caused by some kind of wrong, or injustice. Simple frustration of our wishes should not be a sufficient reason for anger (though people often think it is). As has already been pointed out, the Aristotelian mean is not necessarily moderate: there are times when no anger is appropriate, times when moderate anger is appropriate and times when intense anger is appropriate. Cases of great injustice call for great anger (although what sort of action would then be justified is a further question).

People often struggle with anger – witness the proliferation of anger management courses. An Aristotelian approach would recommend an initial behavioural training coupled with learning to assess whether any given situation warrants anger. As with other virtues, however, our eventual aim should be to come to feel anger appropriately, giving things their proper weight, directing our reactions to the right people and so on.

Another area that often comes up in therapy is the related and vexed issue of assertiveness, in which the extremes are unassertiveness on the one hand and aggression on the other. Here too there is great scope for reflection on how to achieve an appropriate balance: being assertive need not mean transforming oneself from a doormat into an uncaring, selfish monster.

GIVING

Mean: generosity. Deficiency: avarice. Excess: wastefulness.

Generosity concerns the mean in relation to wealth, and in general to things that can be measured in money.[8] In particular, it is about using our money well by giving 'to the right people, in the right amounts, at the right time, and so on'.

What does this mean? Let us imagine that a wealthy man decides, as a result of some tax incentive, to give money to charity. Would we consider him generous? It is probably safe to say that for most people the answer to this question would be no. But let us change the scenario so that instead of tax relief the man gets the admiration and approval

---

[8]There are related uses of the word 'generosity', such as being generous with one's time, but Aristotle restricts the discussion to the monetary kind.

of his new girlfriend, a committed campaigner. Now would we consider him generous? The answer is probably still no. On the other hand, it could be said that as long as he gives of his own money to a worthy cause then he is by definition generous. What else might be required?

Aristotle is quite definite about what that something else is: an attitude of mind. We should give 'with pleasure, or at least without pain'. It is not the act itself of giving, however plentifully, that makes us generous: it is giving with pleasure or at least without begrudging it. It is also giving without ulterior motives, because someone 'who gives to the wrong people . . . or not for the sake of what is noble but for some other reason, will be called not generous but something else' (*NE*, Book IV, Ch. 1). If we are generous we give because we genuinely want to benefit those to whom we give. As before, however, if we realise that we need to become more generous, we have to start by training ourselves to *act* generously.

Generosity is relative to the state of the giver: what is generous for a struggling pensioner will not be so for someone who has won the lottery. According to Aristotle, being generous involves avoiding neglecting our own possessions, or otherwise we should not be able to use them to help other people. On the other hand he thinks that generous people can find it difficult to keep their wealth, since they do not hold it in great regard. And we should not just give to anybody, otherwise we shall not have anything left to give to the right people at the right time and for the right reason. This is a tall order. It seems daunting to try to reconcile all these criteria, which require looking after ourselves and our possessions while giving the right amount to the right people, and therefore balancing our own needs, those of people to whom we have made some kind of commitment, and those of more distant others to whom we are linked only by virtue of our common humanity. It is not possible to come up with absolute rules in this sphere, and these thorny decisions can be made only in relation to particular situations – without forgetting that our attitude is as important as the act of giving.

Virtue ethics is often accused of being self-centred, in that its ultimate aim is the good of the agent. This is true only in a formal sense, however, since the good of the agent includes altruism, or the ability to be concerned about other people's interests and at least sometimes give them precedence over our own. The good of others matters to the virtuous agent because it is the good of others, not because it leads to some kind of self-interest (Annas, 1993).

But why should we be generous or fair at all? While people are known to feel and act altruistically at least sometimes, questions are often raised about how this is possible. We might think that evolution allows no such thing: if our selfish genes (which of course are selfish only metaphorically) gear our behaviour to the aim of self-propagation, it might make sense for us to be altruistic towards our kin – but unrelated others? It is frequently held that there is really no such thing as altruism, and that even if we *appear* to act altruistically we are always in fact motivated by our own self-interest. This position, however, has the unfortunate consequence of obliterating the distinction between altruism and selfishness, which plays an important role in our daily life.

Radcliffe Richards (2000) writes that a certain amount of altruism at the level of individual organisms can fit happily into the 'selfish gene' picture, and that it is possible for evolution to have produced beings with a genuine, though not unlimited, capacity for altruism and sympathy towards others. Even if our genes are (metaphorically) selfish, it does not follow that *we* are.

Aristotle says that generosity applies to taking in the right way as much as giving in the right way. But we could say that it is a different quality altogether – something like fairness – that regulates the sphere of taking appropriately. In this case self-denial (taking less than one's fair share) may be the deficiency and greed (taking more than one's fair share) the excess.

OTHER IMPORTANT SPHERES

Self-regard

The mean here is appropriate pride, while self-deprecation is the deficiency and vanity the excess. Vanity is well exemplified by the character of Gilderoy Lockhart, teacher of Defence Against the Dark Arts at Hogwarts School of Witchcraft and Wizardry in *Harry Potter and the Chamber of Secrets*. Gilderoy struts and preens. He sets his students tests with questions such as:

1. *What is Gilderoy Lockhart's favourite colour?*
2. *What is Gilderoy Lockhart's secret ambition?*
3. *What, in your opinion, is Gilderoy Lockhart's greatest achievement to date?*

Down to:

54. When is Gilderoy Lockhart's birthday, and what would his ideal gift be?

But it is not just the fact that he is so obviously full of himself that makes him a good example of excess in the area of pride. It is also the fact that his view of himself is clearly at odds with reality: when it gets down to performance, Gilderoy Lockhart cannot get the Cornish Pixies back in the cage; he reduces Harry's arm to a boneless appendage when he tries to fix it; and he gets ready to abscond as soon as he is asked to tackle the monster in the Chamber of Secrets.

This is the core feature of this particular excess: rating our achievements and qualities unrealistically highly, considering ourselves more worthy of honour than we actually are. If we wanted to continue the Harry Potter theme, we could say that Dobby, the self-punishing house elf, might be an example of the opposite extreme, self-deprecation (as well as of obsequiousness). The mean in this sphere involves making a proper and accurate assessment of our qualities and worth, in the light of our best evidence. This is not easy, and it demands honest self-examination and the acquisition of self-knowledge.

Success

This triad concerns the importance attributed to success and recognition. The mean in this case might consist in being pleased about the appropriate recognition of our achievements; excess might refer to considering these things so important that more valuable areas of life are neglected or compromised, or being interested in success for its own sake, whether deserved or not and whether conferred by people we respect or not. Overlapping with this is a triad concerning the mean in relation to achievement, where one extreme involves relentlessly driving oneself to greater and greater things, and the other lacking all drive and ambition.

'Toxic success syndrome' (Pearsall, 2002) is a condition said to happen to people who, through their constant striving for success, have reached a state in which they have become unable to appreciate the moment, focus their attention or really connect with those around them. The prescribed cure lies in contentment, calming down and connecting. From an Aristotelian perspective, it is again all about balance: achievement and recognition are goods, and so are contentment and enjoyment of the present. If the two come to clash we will have to reflect on them and willingly follow reason. As has already been discussed, this does not entail that everyone should aim for equal amounts of achievement or contentment, since the mean needs to be worked out in relation to particular individuals and circumstances.

Industriousness

Here the mean involves appropriate effort, avoiding laziness on the one hand and 'workaholism' on the other.

Tenacity

If we have appropriate tenacity we avoid both quitting prematurely and persisting inappropriately.

Guilt and Shame

This sphere is about taking responsibility for our actions, avoiding both unwarranted guilt and blaming others inappropriately. In order to respond appropriately when we have committed some kind of violation, we need to assess the seriousness of our actions and the extent of our personal responsibility. We also need to accept the fact that, as human beings, we are bound to make mistakes. We may need to make amends (Greenberger and Padesky, 1995). But neither all-encompassing guilt nor denial of responsibility for our actions is likely to lead to virtue.

Envy

Finally, we will remember that Aristotle speaks of envy as one of the emotions that are never appropriate. But envy could be used constructively. Essentially, envy is the desire to obtain something that we think we lack and someone else has, and it has been argued that it is possible to regard this as information about what matters to us (de Botton, 2000). When we notice the first stirrings of envy, we should ask ourselves whether there is something that we would like to achieve but so far have not, and whether we can do something to move towards it.

PRACTICAL APPLICATIONS

Aristotle's doctrine of the mean has been accused of being less than helpful in pointing us towards the right thing to do. It is indeed the case that it does not provide us with any ready-made, off-the-shelf rules for how to act. But, as has already been noted, this may be seen as a strength rather than a weakness. It is not possible, given the complexity of human situations, for any rule to fit all circumstances, and it is always in relation to particular situations that an action will be found to be the right or wrong thing to do. It is for this very reason that these themes provide rich material that can be explored and developed through dialogue.

Baggini (2002b, p. 21) sums up these themes: 'First, one has to decide which attitudes and habits to develop and which to suppress. Second, one has to be able to do a bit of thinking on the spot to avoid being rash instead of brave, or wasteful instead of generous. But, nevertheless, it is still true that if we are to live well, we need to develop our characters so that behaving well comes naturally, or else reason will be powerless to overcome our habits.' Human flourishing requires a 'combination of reason and habit' (p. 22). So we may indeed have to feel the fear and do it anyway, feel our anger and not act on it, feel the tendency to be ungenerous and act generously anyway, and so on. But we must remember that this is only the beginning of the journey towards virtue.

In relation to all virtues, we need to address both long-term character issues and immediate situations. In particular, in order to develop our characters we need to:

(1) identify the areas in which we tend to show deficiency or excess and the aspects of our character that we should develop or curb in the light of our reflections on the good life;
(2) make sure we take the relevant considerations into account when making decisions about how to act in those spheres; and
(3) train ourselves to act on the right reasons, so that eventually the right behaviour will come more naturally.

These issues may well find their way into therapy. In relation to the virtues, clients may want to reflect on their character and how they would like to be, and therapists could help them to explore this. Clients often have abstract agendas: they want to be strong, confident, creative (as well as happy, which is what they most want to be) and so on. The problem with these concepts is that they are vague, and therefore do not connect immediately with real life. Making them more precise and concrete is the first step towards assessing the role that they play in the client's life, and one that could be usefully taken in therapy.

The investigation could start from real life examples. The virtue of friendliness, for instance, could be explored by identifying examples in which the client displayed appropriate friendliness, excess or deficiency. From these we can begin to reflect on the general conditions that tend to make friendliness appropriate for the client. This can produce useful action-guiding knowledge (e.g. LeBon, 2001, pp. 144–7).

The following exercises could help to shed light on how the virtues operate in the client's life:

- Make a list of important virtues (such as courage, even temper, appropriate enjoyment of sensual pleasures, generosity, self-respect, and friendliness). To what extent is each virtue expressed in your life? For each virtue, think of recent examples from your daily life that would tend to indicate mean, excess or deficiency.
- What areas of life are you struggling with? What do you think would constitute virtue in that area? Make sure you take into account feedback that you have been given from other people or any other concrete evidence. Monitor the occurrence of excess or deficiency.
- If you tend to lack courage, make a list of things that you are frightened of. For each of these, think about what it is that evokes your fear. Think of instances of justified and unjustified fear. Begin to keep a daily fear diary in order to sharpen your understanding of what kinds of situations tend to be associated with fear. Ask yourself whether it is appropriate on any given occasion.
- If anger is an issue, make a list of things about which you recently got angry. For each of these, think about what it was that made you angry. Was the anger appropriate at all? Was it of the right intensity and directed at the right object? What consequences did it have? Monitor and reflect on the pattern of anger in your life.

Therapists can also help clients to identify methods to deal with inappropriate emotions and establish the right habits. These are covered in the next two chapters.

4

Reasonable Emotions

TWO RECIPES

As we saw in the last chapter, training our emotions is crucial to the development of the virtues. Emotions feature highly on counselling and psychotherapy agendas, especially strong negative ones like fear and anger. People often have difficulties in these areas of their lives and wish to address them in therapy. Different approaches will have different prescriptions as to how to handle troublesome emotions. But it is not uncommon to encounter in the therapy world an outlook according to which feelings and emotions are different in kind from thoughts, almost concrete items that we need to 'get in touch with' and literally 'get out of' ourselves if they cause us problems. It may be thought, for instance, that we can get rid of our anger by screaming or hitting cushions, or of our sadness by crying. Clearly this does not apply to cognitive approaches to therapy, which instead recognise a close connection between emotions and beliefs and are therefore much more akin to the ancient Greek world-view.

Polarised views about the nature and value of emotion exist in psychotherapy and in philosophy. Adhering to one pole or another can have substantial implications for our philosophy of life in general and for how we practise psychotherapy in particular. An Aristotelian 'recipe', according to which emotions can be assessed as appropriate or inappropriate, stands in between two poles that could be called 'stoic' and 'romantic'. I will start by describing these briefly.

1. **The stoic recipe:** to be fully human, we need to eradicate our emotions. This is because human beings are essentially about rationality, and emotions can easily sabotage and hijack the exercise of reason. The best human life, according to this view, is a life of pure reason, a life shorn of emotions to the maximum degree.

- Main advantage: the possibility of achieving a state of tranquillity. If we systematically train ourselves to get rid of our emotions, and succeed, our peace of mind should dramatically increase. This, surely, would be a very positive thing in life, when a more common experience is to be at the mercy of our emotions, which can wreck our serenity, plans and lives. Most people would probably agree that peace of mind is a good thing, well worth striving for.
- Main disadvantages:
  a. Is it possible anyway?
  b. Even if it were possible, could a life devoid of emotions really count as a good, rich human life?
  c. Would we not find it difficult to navigate our way through life without emotions?

2. **The romantic recipe:** to be fully human, we need to yield to our emotions. From this point of view, emotions are what life is all about, and should be embraced and celebrated. The life of pure reason, were it even possible, would be an impoverished and desiccated life, which nobody in their right mind would want to live. Even *trying* to reason about our emotions is vaguely inhuman.
   - Main advantage: a life full of both joys and sorrows would probably be a rich and memorable one.
   - Main disadvantage: being slaves to our emotions would be likely to mean that our life is to some extent out of control. We would find it very difficult to have goals and achieve them, so this would get in the way of other possible ingredients of a good life.

On the one hand there is the potential prize of tranquillity and rationality at the cost of missing out on other important life experiences, and on the other hand a life rich in emotions at the cost of losing all control and peace of mind. This seems like a tough choice. But is it really such a stark choice? Do we really have to choose between a sage-like existence, detached, sheltered from disturbance, and a life of turmoil and lack of restraint? Aristotle would say that we do not. Rationality and peace of mind are good things, and so is a life rich in emotions and experiences. A good life should contain all of these, since they are all part of what makes us uniquely human – with the proviso, however, that reason is in charge to allocate the appropriate value at the appropriate time. The argument is fundamentally about what we should value in life.

In order to start shedding some light on the issue, let us imagine a sudden tragedy: a child dies, say drowned in a river in winter, an unexpected accident. Someone runs to the child's house to break the news, dreading what must be one of the worst tasks in the world. The father opens the door. On hearing the terrible news, he shows no sign of emotion but instead says, quoting Cicero (himself quoting the pre-Socratic philosopher Anaxagoras): 'I was already aware I had begotten a mortal' (Nussbaum, 1994, p. 363; Sorabji, 2000).

The Roman Stoic Epictetus gives the following advice:

> In the case of everything attractive or useful or that you are fond of, remember to say just what sort of thing it is, beginning with the least little things. If you are fond of a jug, say 'I am fond of a jug!' For then when it is broken you will not be upset. If you kiss your child or your wife, say that you are kissing a human being; for when it dies you will not be upset.
>
> (Epictetus, 1983, p. 12)

The Stoic ethos seems nothing but harsh. There is something almost unsavoury about that reaction and that advice. We want to protest that human beings are not like this, and neither should they wish to be. We begin to think of the Stoic sage as a monster, willing to sacrifice his humanity on the altar of rationality and tranquillity. But behind that slightly chilling advice there is a developed and sophisticated theory that deserves exploration.

For the Stoics, nothing apart from our own moral character has real worth. We should not value anything that does not depend on us, because that is too fragile a route to living a good life. Fortune may or may not grant us success, money, health, relationships; but even if it does it could take them away again with no warning. Our own responses to things and events are the only things that truly depend on us. We can strive to achieve all the aforementioned goods, which the Stoics would call 'preferred indifferents' (in a mildly paradoxical turn of phrase), but we should not care about the outcome. Instead, we should concentrate on improving our character, which is all we need to live a good life. The Stoic sage, unlike the Aristotelian one, is self-sufficient in the sense of not needing anything or anybody or any good fortune. Poverty, loneliness, ill-health and even death should be of no consequence.

Hence the kind of advice given above, to practise detachment and withdraw value from things other than our moral character. The Stoics thought that the recommended state of detachment could be achieved by quashing the emotions, which are equated with judgements of value. Things and situations appear good or bad to us, and that is why we respond by seeking them or avoiding them. But we do not have to endorse these beliefs, which are in fact always wrong, since the things we tend to seek or avoid are really neither good nor evil. In order to achieve indifference, therefore, we need to withhold our assent from any thought to the effect that there is something good or bad that has happened or could happen to us. There is no such thing, and the Stoics developed an impressive array of exercises to reinforce that point.

Emotions are thus value judgements. They are faulty judgements, however, since no worldly good is to be valued. If we truly believe this we will have no emotions (or rather, we will have a much smaller range of 'calm' emotions), and this should be our aim. But if this is the price of serenity, it seems very high. Could we really say that we had lived a fully human life in the absence of love, sadness, grief, joy, indignation, hope? There is something seemingly pathological, alien, and anyway generally undesirable, about this prospect. Some eminent scholars, however (Sorabji, 2000; Nussbaum, 2001), have argued that it is possible to separate these different aspects of Stoic doctrine: we can retain the Stoic view of emotions as value judgements and make use of Stoic ideas about how to deal with emotions without having to subscribe to the more demanding theory that nothing in this life should be of value to us apart from our moral character.

ARE EMOTIONS VALUE JUDGEMENTS?

But are emotions value judgements? The question of the nature of emotions has been and still is one of the most intensely debated topics in philosophy and psychology. Many theories have been put forward, but the search for a comprehensive definition has been elusive. To some extent this is due to the fact that the category 'emotion' covers disparate phenomena. Elster (2000) suggests the following pre-analytic classification:

- Shame, contempt, hatred, guilt, anger, pridefulness, liking, pride, admiration (based on a positive or negative evaluation of our own or other people's behaviour or character).
- Envy, indignation, sympathy, pity, malice, gloating (generated by the thought that someone else deservedly or undeservedly possesses something good or bad).

- Joy and grief (generated by the thought of good or bad things that have happened or will happen to oneself).
- Hope, fear, love and jealousy (involving thoughts of good or bad things that may or may not obtain now or in the future).
- Regret, disappointment, relief (involving thoughts about what might have happened or been done).

It seems possible that depending on which of the above we choose to investigate we may come up with entirely different theories. Fear, for instance, may be based on innate biological mechanisms in a way that pride or regret might not be.

Painting with a very broad brush, we could say that through the ages views seem to have clustered around two poles:

1. Emotions are physiological occurrences, non-rational, involuntary, universal, the product of evolutionary processes, similar to what is experienced by other animals.
2. Emotions are cognitive, akin to beliefs, active, susceptible to cultural moulding, different in important ways from what other animals may experience.

BIOLOGICAL ACCOUNTS

This fluctuation from pole to pole has characterised the history of the debate on emotions. William James (2003), for instance, thought of emotions as our perception of physiological changes in the body. He famously argued for a counterintuitive causal connection: we do not cry because we feel sad, we feel sad because we find ourselves crying. The physiological and behavioural reactions to some external event come first, our awareness of them second. This view left cognition out altogether, and was therefore inadequate to explain why emotions tend to change as a result of changes in our thinking.

James's theory was attacked by Cannon (2003), who pointed out that 'visceral' changes (i.e. changes in heart, skin and respiratory and digestive systems) are neither necessary nor sufficient for the occurrence of emotion: it was found that emotional behaviour occurred in animals even when the viscera were isolated from the central nervous system, and conversely that the artificial production of visceral changes did not produce emotion. Cannon also made the important point that the same visceral changes seemed to be associated with different emotions. In order to differentiate between emotions, therefore, it is necessary to identify thoughts and beliefs rather than any physiological occurrences. Schachter and Singer (2003) similarly raised the objection that while physiological arousal (together with cognition) is a necessary element of emotion, it is not on its own sufficient to produce emotion.

Biologically based theories tend to adopt an evolutionary perspective on emotions. From this point of view emotions are seen to fulfil some kind of adaptive purpose, such as detecting events that may affect well-being in a positive or negative way and motivating the relevant behaviour, thereby preserving the individual's interests. According to Ekman (2003), emotions include an appraisal system, set off by environmental events, and a physiological and behavioural 'affect program', which is influenced by experience but primarily has a genetic basis. These processes are viewed as universal. Some evidence for this was sought in the universality of facial expressions associated with emotions: it was found that emotional expressions were interpreted in the same way in literate and pre-literate cultures (Ekman, 2003). It could be argued, however, that this interpretation applies only to a basic set of emotions such as anger, fear, disgust, surprise, sadness and joy. More complex emotions, like grief, are harder to explain through this lens, and we may have to resort to explaining these away as either a non-functional side-effect of some function or a hereditary remnant of something that was at some past point useful (Frijda, 2003).

An influential modern theory presenting a biological and evolutionary viewpoint was put forward by Joseph LeDoux (1998). According to LeDoux, the category 'emotion' might turn out to be illusory and be found to encompass different neural systems that have evolved for different reasons. The systems that generate emotional behaviours are automatic and highly preserved through evolution, so that in humans they are likely to be similar to those present in other animals (e.g. systems for protection against danger and responding to it quickly). When these unconscious systems operate in creatures that have the capacity for conscious awareness, emotional feelings may occur. LeDoux's own work has focused on fear. He has shown that there are two brain pathways for fear. One is pre-programmed and automatic and bypasses higher processing systems. This is rough and ready, and has the advantage of speed but the disadvantage of crudeness. The other involves higher processing systems and is therefore more accurate, but at the cost of being slower.

Although LeDoux has shown that at least some forms of fear may be triggered automatically by perceptual or sensory stimuli, it is problematic to generalise from these findings to all human emotions. Elster (2000) points out that 'in societies that have moved beyond the struggle for survival, major emotional experiences tend to have complex cognitive antecedents' (p. 33) and so would not fit easily into this mould.

COGNITIVE ACCOUNTS

These tend to see emotions as resulting from, or equivalent to, thoughts and beliefs. Physiological occurrences without beliefs are not seen as emotions. As Calhoun (2003, p. 240) puts it, for cognitive approaches 'fear minus a belief in danger is not fear'. This is the converse of James's view that if we subtracted physiological disturbance from fear all we would have left would be a cool belief in danger rather than an emotion. Beliefs seem necessary to individuate and differentiate between emotions.

To see this, try the following thought experiment: imagine that your heart had suddenly started to flutter wildly and you felt dizzy and had a peculiar sense that it was as if a vortex were opening underneath you and swallowing you. You had not ingested any drugs, legal or otherwise, prior to this. What would you think and do? My guess is that you would think you were being taken ill and reach for the phone to get in touch with a doctor as quickly as you could. On the other hand, if this experience occurred after you had received the news that someone you loved had died you could begin to identify it as an emotion. And you would identify it as a different emotion if this happened after finding out that you had won the lottery.

A physiological experience without any object and any value judgement is not an emotion. We can tell emotions apart only by identifying judgements, not sensations. Conversely, it is possible to be, say, very angry in the absence of any physical sensations whatsoever. This is not the most typical instance, of course, but it is by no means bizarre or incomprehensible. The anger is in our thoughts.

And yet, cognitive accounts can seem paradoxical. We are used to thinking of emotions as experiences that we undergo rather than actively choose, often in opposition to rational assessment, and about which we seem to be able to do little or nothing. All this differs greatly from beliefs, that we tend to associate with rationality, choice and responsibility.

Some of the puzzles raised by cognitive accounts are identified by Hursthouse (1999):

1. Sometimes emotions clash with beliefs, as is the case when people are aware that an emotion is irrational and yet still feel it. This would seem to indicate that emotions are different from beliefs.
2. If we subscribe to this kind of account we will have to either attribute judgements and beliefs to toddlers and animals or say that they have no emotions, neither of which seems plausible.

But 'cognitive' does not have to refer to fully-fledged, explicit, verbalised beliefs, as a number of authors point out. Hursthouse (1999) writes that the essential aspect of emotions is that they involve ideas of 'good' and 'evil', in the sense of objects of pursuit and avoidance. Calhoun (2003) differentiates 'cognitive sets' from belief systems: while the latter are 'reflectively held, articulable judgments', the former are 'prereflectively held, originally unarticulated systems' (p. 244), which may be passively acquired. Fully conceptualised and articulated beliefs form a small part of our cognitive life, which for the major part includes 'an unarticulated framework for interpreting the world, which, if articulated, would be an enormous network of claims not all of which would be accepted by the individual as his beliefs' (p. 244). Strictly speaking, it is not beliefs but certain ways of 'seeing as' that are constituents of emotions. This view can account for discrepancies between beliefs and emotions and can allow toddlers and animals to have emotions.

Lazarus (2003) also tries to pinpoint the minimum cognitive requirements for an emotion to occur. He concludes that an emotion is a perception that something in a person's environment is relevant to the person's well-being: there are personal goals at stake, and the relationship with the environment involves either harm or benefit. If the former, the emotion will be negative; if the latter it will be positive. This appraisal – whether conscious or not – that a relevant goal is at stake is the minimum cognitive condition for the occurrence of an emotion.

The particular understanding of what 'cognitive' means seems important in this respect, since depending on this we may find theorists agreeing or disagreeing. There seems to be a fair amount of agreement, for instance, about the view that emotions are based on some kind of appraisal of how events in the world affect the organism's well-being. The disagreement appears to be mainly about the extent to which this appraisal involves higher cognitive processes.

IS THERE SUCH A THING AS 'EMOTION'?

Some authors draw sceptical conclusions from the existence of such different views. According to Elster (1999, p. 246) there are seven main characteristics of what he calls 'occurrent' emotions, i.e. actual episodes of, say, anger and fear:[9]

1. Qualitative feel.
2. Cognitive antecedents.
3. An intentional object (they are *about* something).
4. Physiological arousal.
5. Physiological expressions (such as posture, voice pitch, blushing, smiling, frowning, crying).
6. Valence on the pleasure–pain dimension.
7. Characteristic action tendencies.

Elsewhere (2000), Elster adds three more possible features, i.e. sudden onset, unbidden occurrence (i.e. the fact that they tend to be undergone rather than chosen) and brief duration. These, however, have many counterexamples. He concludes that 'the features most robustly associated with the emotions are those of unbidden occurrence, cognitive antecedents, intentional objects, arousal, action tendencies, and valence' (p. 42).

But even these are not always present in what we intuitively class as emotions. Cognitive antecedents, for instance, seem to be missing in the instances of fear investigated by LeDoux (1998),[10] as already discussed. An intentional object may be missing from emotions experienced in relation to music – although we may *stipulate* that if an intentional object is missing the experience is to be regarded as a mood rather than an emotion. Some emotions in particular, such as regret and sympathy, tend to lack concomitant physiological arousal, and even the ones that are usually associated with it (e.g. anger) may occur without it. Characteristic facial expressions are reliably associated with emotions such as joy, anger and fear but not with others (e.g. guilt, shame, hope, pride, envy, regret). Not all emotions have specific action

---

[9]These are contrasted with 'dispositional' emotions, i.e. the *tendency* to have a particular emotion.

[10]Although, as Nussbaum (2001) points out, there is a sense in which cognitive processes (in the sense of receiving and processing information) *are* already involved in the kind of mechanisms described by LeDoux.

tendencies (e.g. pride, relief, regret, sadness, disappointment), and these may be suppressed. Elster also questions the necessary association of emotions with pleasure and pain. From these reflections he concludes that we should think of the features listed above as characteristic properties, typically rather than necessarily present.

Elster (2000) writes that the category 'emotion' may be a faulty one, which turns out to correspond to nothing really existing in nature. Similarly, LeDoux (1998) comments that 'emotion' may turn out not to refer to any one phenomenon, and that it is more likely that different emotions are mediated by different brain networks, functioning differently. According to Griffiths (2003), 'emotion' is nothing but a folk psychology term that does not refer to any real object of scientific study. This does not mean that there is nothing going on when people experience an emotion, only that the category 'emotion' does not shed any light on what it is.

It is suggested that the term 'emotion' may in this respect be similar to the discredited category of 'superlunary objects' (Griffiths, 2003, p. 285): 'There really are objects outside the orbit of the moon, but the category of the "superlunary" is as arbitrary a way of grouping objects together as it is possible to devise. There is no such thing in nature as a distinction between the superlunary and the sublunary realms. . . . Similarly, the idea that we need a theory of the emotions, or a theory of some specific emotion, may be a mistake.' While this may turn out to be right, there does seem to be a sense in which 'emotion' has more of an essential link with our lived experience than a 'superlunary object'. While the latter category could be easily dispensed with in our daily life, emotion terms would be a lot more difficult to do without.

There is certainly much to be sceptical about in relation to the emotions. And it seems plausible to say that, depending on which emotion we choose to study, we may end up with different pictures of what an emotion is. While a picture of emotions as hardwired products of evolution could happily apply to fear, it may not apply equally to emotions based on complex beliefs. Nussbaum (2001) brings together all the relevant evidence in her enlightened cognitive perspective, presented in the next section.

A NEO-STOIC ACCOUNT

Nussbaum eloquently and convincingly presents her revised Stoic views in a number of books and papers (1993, 1994, 1995, 2001). As has already been pointed out, she subscribes to a version of the Stoic theory that emotions are value judgements, without further agreeing with the view that nothing in life should have value apart from our own moral character. According to Nussbaum (2001, p. 22), emotions are 'forms of evaluative judgment that ascribe to certain things and persons outside a person's own control great importance for the person's own flourishing'. They have the following features:

1. They have an object: they are *about* something. They would not be identifiable as emotions without this. More diffuse emotions, lacking an object, are best seen as moods. In practice, however, it may be difficult to distinguish between moods and those emotions whose object is vague.
2. The object is perceived in a certain way, from a particular point of view. This perception may or may not be accurate; in fact the object may not even exist. This is important, since 'What distinguishes fear from hope, fear from grief, love from hate – is not so much the identity of the object . . . but the way the object is perceived: in fear, as a threat, but with some chance for escape, in hope, as in some uncertainty, but with a chance for a good outcome, in grief as lost, in love as invested with a special sort of radiance' (2003, p. 276).
3. They embody complex beliefs about the object. These are essential in identifying and discriminating between emotions. Taking some examples from Aristotle's *Rhetoric*, she writes that fear requires us to believe that 'bad events are impending', that they are 'seriously bad', that we are not 'in a position to ward them off'; on the other hand, that 'our fate is not sealed', but that 'there is still some uncertainty about what may befall'. For anger we must believe that there has been some damage to us or someone close to us, that the damage is 'not trivial but significant', that it was done 'by someone . . . [and] done willingly'; that 'it would be right for the perpetrator . . . to be punished' (2003, p. 276).
4. They involve some attribution of value to the object, which is considered important to our life and our flourishing in some way. Nussbaum (2001) describes emotions as 'eudaimonistic', implicitly acknowledging that as human beings we are simply not self-sufficient. By accepting these judgements of value we allow ourselves and our good to be dependent on things outside our control. But, unlike the Stoics, Nussbaum considers this a crucial part of being human.

According to Nussbaum (2001), the emotion is identical with the value judgement. This may seem counterintuitive, but it becomes understandable if her theory is spelled out more fully. Since we are embodied beings, emotions will typically involve bodily sensations and changes; but this does not mean that the ascription of emotion would or should be withdrawn if these other constituents were to be missing. If the *judgement* were to be withdrawn, on the other hand, so, typically, would the ascription of emotion.

The value judgements that occur in emotions are different from other kinds of judgements in the sense that they are accompanied by 'rich and dense perceptions of the object, which are highly concrete and replete with detail' (p. 65). The evaluative content alone does not capture the experience of emotion: in grief, for instance, the understanding that a person dear to us is dead also involves 'a storm of memories and concrete perceptions that swarm around that content, but add more than is present in it' (p. 65). We are 'perceiving creatures', and our sensory abilities give emotions their 'rich texture' (p. 65).

In Nussbaum's (2001) particular brand of cognitive theory, then, emotions are 'cognitive' in the sense of being importantly involved in taking in and evaluating information about the world. The judgements involved, however, are not necessarily explicit or verbal. And an emotion is not just any kind of belief, since it involves an attitude towards an object that is considered in some way important to the individual's flourishing. Like all cognitive processes, emotions are also bodily processes, and are typically associated with embodied phenomena such as bodily changes, perceptions, imaginings and a 'feel'. But physiological information does not need to be written into the definition of emotion. Nussbaum considers her theory to be well placed to account for two apparently non-cognitive features of emotions, i.e. their urgency and the sense of passivity before them. The former is due to the fact that they concern important goals and projects, and the latter to the fact that their objects are outside our control.

This view accommodates the ability of animals and young children to have emotions, since they are capable of 'intentionality, selective attention and appraisal' (2001, p. 91). It is also compatible with the existence of cultural variation. Nussbaum (2001) writes that some emotions are bound to be universal, since our common biology entails vulnerabilities and attachments that as human beings we can hardly fail to have. We are all likely to experience some form of anger, hope, grief, attachment and compassion, for instance. But social variation does indeed exist, and some of its sources include: physical conditions; metaphysical, religious and cosmological beliefs; local practices; and language (pp. 152–7). Importantly, Nussbaum also acknowledges that emotions may be influenced by childhood experiences, which can lead to perceiving present objects through the filter of the past.

Although this is a neo-Stoic account, it could equally well be a neo-Aristotelian one: while Aristotle's theory of emotion was not fully spelled out, emotions were certainly regarded as connected with beliefs; and, as we have seen, he considered many things valuable in life. As well as virtuous action, it is appropriate for instance to care about friends, family, and one's own life and health. Emotions are always rational in the descriptive sense that they are in some way cognitive and therefore subject to rational assessment. They are not, however, always rational in the normative sense of conforming to some notion of the right way to reason (Nussbaum, 2001). In this latter sense they are often irrational. Our task is that of sorting emotional responses into those that point to real value in the world, and should be heeded, and those that do not, which should be curbed.

TRANQUILLITY OR STRAWBERRIES?

If emotions can usefully be seen as value judgements, then the question is what we should value. While the Stoics had recommended that we value no worldly goods, Russell had the following advice for a good life, encouraging us to value as many things as possible:

> Suppose one man likes strawberries and another does not; in what respect is the latter superior? There is no abstract and impersonal proof either that strawberries are good or that they are not good. To the man who likes them they are good; to the man who dislikes them they are not. But the man who likes them has a pleasure which the other does not have; to that extent his life is more enjoyable and he is better adapted to the world in which both must live ... The more things a man is interested in, the more opportunities of happiness he has, and the less he is at the mercy of fate, since if he loses one thing he can fall back on another.
>
> (Russell, 1975, pp. 123–4)

Some things in the world are to be valued. Emotions are an expression of this, and are therefore an intrinsic part of a good human life. Accepting this means allowing ourselves to be deeply affected by outside circumstances, and therefore giving up a certain amount of control. But emotions should not be valued to the extent that our life becomes unmanageable, as it would if we were not able to keep them in check when necessary – if they interfered with other important goals, for instance, including that of being a rational human being. We should be able to embrace or curb an emotion depending on whether it is appropriate or inappropriate, which takes us back to Aristotle and aiming for the mean. We need to learn to make sound decisions as to when to give priority to tranquillity or strawberries.

THE SLIPPERY SLOPE ARGUMENT

At this point the Stoic could say to the Aristotelian that if we allow emotions at all they are bound to get out of control. That is their nature. We are deceiving ourselves if we think that we can manage them: there can be no rationality without full eradication.

But slippery slope arguments are often misleading. As Warburton (1996) puts it, they tend to 'obscure the fact that the descent towards the worst possible scenario is by no means inevitable'. If we take this kind of reasoning to its exaggerated extreme 'it would seem to follow that if we eat at all we are in serious danger of eating more and more until we end up obese; if we tell a small white lie we will end up by betraying our country' (p. 109), and so on. Therefore we need accurate information about the likelihood of the descent occurring before making such predictions. In the case of emotions there would seem to be some rationale for the warning, since violent emotions do seem to impair our capacity for cool reasoning. But this is by no means an inevitability. If we notice that we are accelerating too fast we can resolve to shift into a lower gear, or apply the brakes.

Aristotle did not believe in the slippery slope. It is appropriate to care about things in the world (friends, family, life, health). It is appropriate to feel emotions (fear at the prospect of our own death, grief for the death of someone dear to us and so on). Those things are part of the good life, and so are our emotions. But our attributions of value could be wildly inappropriate and need to be educated.

ARE EMOTIONS HELPFUL?

Seneca's (2003, p. 14) vivid description of the symptoms displayed by the angry man is designed to reinforce the point that emotions are bad for us: 'eyes ablaze and glittering, a deep flush over all the face as blood boils up from the vitals, quivering lips, teeth pressed together, bristling hair standing on end, breath drawn in and hissing, the crackle of writhing limbs, groans and bellowing, speech broken off with the words barely uttered, hands struck together too often, feet stamping the ground, the whole body in violent motion "menacing mighty

wrath in mien," the hideous horrifying face of swollen self-degrada-
tion – you would hardly know whether to call the vice hateful or
ugly.'

But emotions can be a positive *or* a negative force in our life. Here
are some ways in which emotions can be helpful:

- they can give us an initial (but fallible) indication of where value
  might lie, of what to seek and what to avoid;
- they can help us to make decisions by directing our attention to the
  most important features of a situation;
- they can help communication with others;
- they can motivate us to act.

And some ways in which emotions can be unhelpful:

- they can impair reasoning in general;
- they can impair decision-making in particular;
- they can lead to irrational action.

This reminds me of a time when I consulted a book on houseplants
for a diagnosis on some ailing plant or other, and on looking up the
symptoms I learned that they may be due either to overwatering or to
underwatering. 'Yes,' I puzzled, 'but which?'

The neurologist Antonio Damasio (1994) has been a vocal defender
of the usefulness of emotions in decision-making. Damasio observed
that people whose emotional functioning had become impaired as a
result of neurological damage were also negatively affected in their
ability to make decisions, and he posited a causal connection between
the two (it should be noted that this causal link has been questioned:
compare, for example, Elster, 2000; Nussbaum, 2001). According to
Damasio there is a distinction between primary emotions, which are
innate and hardwired, and more complex secondary emotions. He also
differentiates between an emotion, which is the collection of changes
in body state, and a feeling, i.e. the experience of those changes (in
juxtaposition with the relevant mental images) in animals that have
consciousness, such as humans.

Emotions and feelings help us to make decisions by directing and
focusing our attention on to some features of our environment rather
than others, thereby eliminating or prioritising available options.
Without emotions we would not know how to rank all the stimuli that
we encounter. Emotions are in this way a kind of compass that guides

us towards areas of importance in life. As Damasio (1994) acknowledges, however, emotions are just as likely to impair our decision-
making ability: while 'certain aspects of the process of emotion and
feeling are indispensable for rationality' (p. xiii), it is also the case that
'emotions and feelings can cause havoc in the processes of reasoning
under certain circumstances' (p. xii); and even when they play a positive role 'they do not do the deciding for us' (p. xii): they simply 'take
us to the appropriate place in a decision-making space, where we may
put the instruments of logic to good use' (p. xiii). The operation of
emotions and feelings may reduce the number of options to consider,
but these still need to be assessed rationally.

According to Frijda (2003), emotions are generally useful: in particular, their function is to 'signal events that are relevant to the individual's concerns, and to motivate behavior to deal with those events'
(p. 141). They can, however, go badly wrong, and result in 'phobic fears
and panics, guilt emotions without clear causes in social transgression
or neglect, panics and states of desperation in clinical depressions, and
unfounded jealousies' (p. 136). Elster (2000) writes that 'The feeling
of urgency bestowed by many emotions . . . can interfere with rational
acquisition of information. In extreme cases the action tendency associated with the emotion may blot out considerations of other options and
of long-term consequences' (p. 165).

Emotions can help or hinder. In this respect we should remind ourselves again of Aristotle's clear warning that precision is not to be
sought or found in this arena. There can be no rulebook providing a
neat classification of all the cases in which a particular emotion is or is
not appropriate. If there were one, it would be more like the book on
houseplants: it is only by looking at particular situations that we can
assess whether an emotion is helping or hindering, whether we should
endorse it or curb it. In order for the emotions to play a positive role
in our life we need to learn to recognise whether they are appropriate
in relation to specific circumstances.

There is some agreement on the main ways in which emotions may
be inappropriate. De Sousa (2003) reports that emotions may be inappropriate in kind and degree. Similarly, Ben Ze'ev (2000) considers
emotions to be harmful '(1) when they are applied in circumstances
that are not suited to the given emotion, and (2) when they are excessive' (p. 173). And according to Seeburger (1997), emotions can fail to
fit the situation in which they occur either by being the wrong emotion
for the situation in question or by being out of proportion. More specifically in relation to Aristotle, Sorabji (2000) says that 'What is

required for good temper, courage, temperance, or self-esteem is the right amount, timing, and direction of anger, fear, pleasure, or pride' (p. 194).

We could sum this up by saying that an emotion is inappropriate if:

1. it has the wrong object altogether; or
2. it is out of proportion (being either excessive or deficient).

The view that emotions may be assessed as appropriate or inappropriate should not be equated with the view that they are to be entirely ruled by reason. This is clearly inadequate to account for the complexity of the relationships between 'cool' calculative reason and the emotions, which could be regarded as cognitive states that have closer connections with what have been called 'visceral factors' (i.e. states that involve strong physiological changes, such as hunger, thirst and pain) (Elster, 2000). The emotions play an important role in the detection of value and therefore in decision-making; on the other hand, being strongly associated with beliefs, emotions are themselves subject to rational assessment.

Solomon (1999) argues against any world-view that tears reason apart from emotion and puts it on a pedestal. However, his ideal of the 'passionate life' is hardly an advocacy of giving free rein to our wildest instincts with no regard for reason. Instead, he recognises that 'There are emotions that are out of the range of virtue (for instance, envy), and there are degrees or intensities of emotion . . . that are by no means virtuous' (p. 21). Emotions are 'rational insofar as they "fit," if they are appropriate, if someone else could articulate reasons to support them even if the subject cannot do so him- or her[self]' (p. 82). But this assessment can be made only on the basis of a 'detailed analysis of the conditions for rational (warranted) anger, and jealousy, and love, and grief' (p. 84).

Anger, for instance, involves judgements of blame, but a lot can go wrong in making this assessment: we can be wrong about the facts or about 'the harm done or the blameworthiness of the person with whom one is angry'; or we can be 'right about the facts and justified about the warrant for anger, yet go wrong in its expression, misdirecting it . . . or overdoing it' (Solomon, 1999, p. 84). Similarly, fear involves 'the recognition of a danger, and one can be wrong about the danger, its imminence or gravity' (p. 85). And so on for all the other emotions.

EMOTIONAL MANAGEMENT

One of the characteristic abilities of human beings is that of making a distinction between appearance and reality. A simple instance of this is the case mentioned by Aristotle and discussed by Nussbaum (2003): although the sun looks to us as if it were about a foot wide, we know that it is in fact very large, and we are therefore able to reject the appearance. This kind of case is uncontroversial. Other cases may be harder to settle, and especially so in relation to the emotions.

A Greek Stoic, Chrysippus, advocated asking ourselves two diagnostic questions on noticing the first stirrings of an emotion:

1. Is there good or bad at hand? (As we have seen, the answer to this question for the Stoics was practically always negative.)
2. Is it appropriate to react? (This was a handy technique for people who fell short of full Stoic sainthood: even if we wrongly believe that something bad has happened, we can still realise that certain reactions are not appropriate because of their negative consequences.)

Taking our inspiration from Chrysippus, and in the light of the previous discussion, we could adopt the following diagnostic questions:

1. Does the emotion fit the situation?
2. Is the degree of the emotion appropriate to the situation?
3. Is it appropriate to react?
4. If so, how?

The attitude we need to encourage in ourselves is one of listening to our emotions, since they will undoubtedly be saying something about our relationship with the world around us. But this something may express accurate information or be a wildly distorted perception. We should suspend our endorsement of an emotion until we have probed into it to ascertain the extent to which it is appropriate to the situation: is our anger misdirected, or excessive? Our jealousy or fear unfounded? Our guilt unwarranted? If an emotion is found to be inappropriate it will need to be managed.

'Emotional regulation, or management, refers to any initiative we take to influence which emotions we have, when we have them, and how we experience and express these emotions' (Ben Ze'ev, 2000, p. 221). Signs that some emotional management may be in order include an emotion's being at odds with our judgement, for instance, or having a negative impact on our life. Emotional management may also be seen as the first step towards virtue and the good life. According to Elster (2000, pp. 164–5): 'Although emotions themselves cannot be chosen, one can affect them indirectly by seeking out or avoiding the conditions under which they occur, by giving in to or resisting their characteristic expressions, and by cultivating dispositions to have them.'

Emotions may be modified over time by monitoring and managing their occurrence. If we tend to get angry a lot, for instance, it may not be open to us to turn ourselves into models of even temper overnight. What we can do is start controlling some aspect of our experience of anger, in the hope that the changes we introduce will become more natural with practice. We could learn to refrain from behaviours such as shouting at people, stamping our feet and slamming doors, or we could challenge our reasons to be angry, or consider the consequences of our angry behaviour.

It is interesting to consider whether the expression of a strong negative emotion is likely to be harmful or beneficial. In the heyday of humanistic psychotherapy it had become something of a dogma that 'getting emotions out' was a good thing. The limitations of such a 'psychohydraulic' outlook have already been pointed out. And contrary to that view, it would seem that, far from eliminating an emotion, outward manifestation may serve only to fuel it, whereas control may allow it to wither.

According to Seligman (2003), we have learned to believe the psychodynamic theory that 'If we don't express our rage, it will come out elsewhere – even more destructively, as in cardiac disease. But this theory turns out to be false; in fact, the reverse is true. Dwelling on trespass and the expression of anger produces more cardiac disease and more anger' (p. 69). Seligman reports that the expression of anger tends to raise rather than lower blood pressure. He also writes that 'emotions, left to themselves, will dissipate' (p. 70). As a corrective to this, we need to consider the possibility that in some instances a constant curbing of the manifestation of an emotion in the absence of attempts to manage it in other ways (e.g. through challenging our beliefs) or change the circumstances associated with it, could lead to an intensified expression later.

From this perspective, working with emotions means viewing them as fallible indicators of value, and helping clients to explore whether the value that is initially perceived is real or due to some kind of distortion. This work needs to be placed in the context of the good life and the virtues. We can undertake a joint investigation to find out whether an emotion fits the situation in kind and degree and what kind of reaction – if any – may be warranted. If distortion is identified, we can assist the client in monitoring and managing the emotion in one of a number of ways. It is possible that the simple act of questioning whether an emotion is appropriate in kind or degree will, by challenging the previous point of view, dissolve or transform the emotion. But often a little more effort is required.

PRACTICAL APPLICATIONS

For many ancient schools of philosophy (Hellenistic and Roman in particular), as Hadot (1995) reports, philosophy was not 'a theoretical construct, but . . . a method for training people to live and to look at the world in a new way' (p. 107); it did not 'consist in teaching an abstract theory . . . but rather in the art of living' (p. 83). This perspective was lost in the Middle Ages, when philosophy became subsidiary to theology and the more practical, life-transforming aspects of it 'were relegated to Christian mysticism and ethics' (p. 107). Hadot calls these practical methods 'spiritual exercises' because he considers this expression to encompass the role of imagination in a way that 'thought exercises', for instance, would not. For the Stoics, who made great use of exercises, these were aimed at extirpating the passions. Generally, exercises were seen as an important part of supporting the difficult project of character transformation.

Aristotle's ethics was also conceived as a very practical enterprise, which could be described as a training in the art of living. While Aristotelian exercises are not as well attested as Stoic ones, Sorabji (2000) writes that the exercises used by ancient schools were to some extent interchangeable between schools despite doctrinal differences. Clearly in an Aristotelian context exercises would be aimed at the modulation rather than extirpation of the emotions and at the cultivation of the virtues.

The rest of this chapter describes a number of techniques to apply to ourselves or with clients if, on the basis of our answers to the above questions and our diagnosis of the situation, we conclude that emotional management is required. I will borrow methods from Stoics and Epicureans as well as from modern therapies. Cognitive–behavioural schools of psychotherapy, such as cognitive–behaviour therapy (CBT) and rational–emotive behaviour therapy (REBT), also employ cognitive and behavioural techniques to deal with emotions, albeit in a different context. The founder of rational–emotive behaviour therapy,

Albert Ellis, is fond of saying that his views were influenced by Stoicism. To be sure, there are many differences between the two, but the idea that we can change the way we feel by changing our beliefs does have Stoic origins – although it was common to a number of Greek philosophical schools, including Aristotle's.

EXAMINING THE EVIDENCE FOR OUR BELIEFS

Cognitive–behaviour therapies regard emotions as mediated by beliefs: it is not events in the world that disturb us, it is how we think about those events. This is captured in the so-called ABC model:

A = activating event
B = belief, and
C = consequences (emotional or behavioural).

Disruptive emotions are seen as the result of automatic negative thoughts that are difficult to even detect, let alone change. These in turn are often affected by core beliefs, or long-standing inflexible views about ourselves, others and the world. A cognitive–behaviour therapist might instruct a client to monitor the links among situations, thoughts and emotions, to spot the emotionally charged thoughts, and to replace irrational beliefs with rational ones. Distress at the thought of not being appreciated professionally, for instance, may be dealt with by questioning the evidence for that negative belief and seeking evidence to support alternative beliefs, thereby arriving at a more balanced view, based on a consideration of all the evidence.

QUESTIONING THE SIGNIFICANCE OF AN OBJECT

1. In the case of someone being distressed because she thought that she had made a fool of herself at a social occasion and was therefore disliked, an REBT therapist might say something like: 'Even if people did dislike you, how would that be awful? OK, it is not pleasant, and it is better when people like us, but it is hardly a law of the universe that you must always be liked.' Such a point of view may be therapeutic despite initially sounding most cruel. For REBT, strong negative emotions are always unhealthy.
2. The technique of reframing aims to instigate a different perspective on things, to invest situations with a new meaning. A good example of reframing is the story of a woman, a compulsive cleaner, who was

alienating her husband and sons through her obsessive carpet cleaning. She would vacuum several times a day and was determined to eliminate any little dent in the carpet as soon as it appeared. The therapist used the following intervention:

'I want you to close your eyes and see your carpet, and see that there is not a single footprint on it anywhere. It's clean and fluffy – not a mark anywhere.' The woman was smiling and enjoying this fantasy, when the therapist continued: '*And realize fully that that means that you are totally alone, and that people you care for and love are nowhere around.*' The woman began to feel terrible. 'Now, put a few footprints there and look at those footprints and know that the people you care most about in the world are nearby'.

(Bandler and Grinder, 1982, p. 6)

The meaning of the dents in the carpet was thereby dramatically transformed.

3. Epictetus' advice on how to prepare for and deal with loss, already quoted, is also relevant here. While we may consider this harsh and have reservations about using it to deal with grief and bereavement, it may well come in handy when in danger of becoming excessively attached and/or overreacting to the loss of jugs (or cars, or other material possessions).

In the case of everything attractive or useful or that you are fond of, remember to say just what sort of thing it is, beginning with the least little things. If you are fond of a jug, say 'I am fond of a jug!' For then when it is broken you will not be upset.

(Epictetus, 1983, p. 12)

4. A more general technique is that of asking ourselves what is up to us and what is not. If something is not up to us we should not be concerned about it. This could be useful even if we disagree with the Stoics on what it is reasonable to value, because surely if something is totally beyond our control, we should endeavour not to get unduly distressed about it. The Serenity Prayer encapsulates this outlook. It may be difficult to say with precision what can or cannot be changed, but some things we can be sure of: we cannot change the past, for instance, therefore we should not spend too much time wishing vwe could – what we should do instead is to learn from our past experiences.

DIVERTING OUR ATTENTION

1. The Epicureans advocated the technique of diverting our thoughts from a painful situation by remembering good things from the past. Shifting our attention at times of distress, though not necessarily by thinking of the past, is a useful technique, which could be used any time we want to discourage a harmful emotion.

   In the literature on *flow* (Csikszentmihalyi, 1997), it is stressed that the ability to direct our attention is *the* fundamental skill in life. This is because attention acts as a kind of filter between us and the world, and the experiences we have are to a large extent moulded by how we control it. Giving painful emotions too much attention somehow makes them more real, and when we are in the grip of a negative emotion we may not be in the best position to reason calmly about the situation and decide what to do about it. At these times we need to learn to reallocate our attention. This could be done in various ways.

   We could, for instance, follow the Epicureans' advice about thinking of good things from the past – or from the present, for that matter. But many diverting techniques are behavioural: we could garden, play the piano, exercise, walk, work, paint; even listening to someone else's problems could do the trick. When we return to the original situation, we may find that it has acquired a slightly different look, and is somehow less raw, more manageable. Then we can start to think about possible solutions. On the other hand, we could overdo it: feeling consistently distressed about something is a sign that something is amiss and needs to be dealt with. Denying this is rarely beneficial.

2. Thought stopping. This is a well-known behavioural technique that consists in simply giving ourselves the instruction to 'stop' whenever the thoughts associated with the unwanted emotion occur.

3. Neurolinguistic programming advocates the use of various techniques for mentally manipulating the object of the unwanted emotion. These include such tricks as turning the volume down, making the image fuzzy or distorting the image.

LETTING IT PASS

It has been suggested that emotions like anger and fear follow a set pattern, which is similar for all impulses. These are: '(1) onset, (2) increase, (3) peak, (4) decrease, and (5) cessation' (Seeburger, 1997,

p. 66). Most of the time we find these emotions so distressing that we are driven to react quickly to get rid of them. And of course in many cases we may be perfectly justified in doing so. But at other times we need to train ourselves to sit the emotion out, in the sure knowledge that if we just wait the impulse or emotion will eventually disappear. This is a rather meditative approach to dealing with emotions. Instead of actively manipulating our thinking or our actions, we observe the process without getting involved in the content. We let an emotion be without either acting on it or denying it. This, perhaps paradoxically, can be a very effective way of changing it.

Attending to our experience, including our emotions, is the foundation of Buddhist mindfulness meditation (which of course is much more than just a technique for dealing with emotions). Stephen Batchelor writes, in relation to hatred:

> To embrace hatred is to accept it for what it is: a disruptive but transient state of mind. Awareness observes it jolt into being, coloring consciousness and gripping the body. The heart accelerates, the breathing becomes shallow and jagged, and an almost physical urge to react dominates the mind. At the same time, this frenzy is set against a dark, quiet gulf of hurt, humiliation, and shame. Awareness notices all this without condoning or condemning, repressing or expressing. It recognizes that just as hatred arises, so it will pass away.
>
> (Batchelor, 1998, p. 60)

ADOPTING THE RIGHT ATTITUDE TOWARDS THE FUTURE

One Stoic technique for dealing with excessive attachment to things outside our control is to anticipate misfortune so as to be prepared when loss occurs. The good Stoic should vividly imagine poverty, death and suffering (Hadot, 1995). The Epicureans held the opposite view, that it is helpful to entertain hope of future pleasures.

There are dangers in both these approaches to the future. Considering possible future misfortunes can have the benefit of preparing us for these should they occur. But unless we couple this practice with wider principles to the effect that the value of what we might lose is only apparent, it is more likely to lead to depression than to tranquillity.

'Positive thinking' on the other hand can have the benefit of promoting a state of mind conducive to the achievement of our goals: if we expect good things to happen, we are more likely to act in ways that will actually realise them. But, apart from encouraging a certain amount of wishful thinking, this approach has the drawback of leaving us vulnerable to disappointment if, owing to circumstances beyond our control, the hoped-for future does not materialise.

While less well known than positive thinking, 'defensive pessimism' (Norem, 2002) encourages a more realistic attitude: instead of wallowing in rosy-tinted fantasies, thinking about worst-case scenarios can help us to do our best by preparing for the worst.

A balanced approach to the future is embodied in another Stoic practice, which has been described as 'wanting and expecting with reservation'. This has more of an Aristotelian ring to it, and entailed qualifying wishes and expectations with expressions like 'if Zeus wills' or 'if nothing prevents' (Sorabji, 2000, p. 219).

We should allow ourselves to aim for and expect good things, but in the full realisation that life comes with no guarantees and that disappointment is a ubiquitous experience.

ACTING 'AS IF'

This is another well-known method, which, as the name implies, entails acting as if we already possessed certain attitudes that we are in fact still developing. This could be frowned upon and condemned as false and inauthentic. But, as has been discussed, changing engrained habits tends to involve a phase in which the new attitudes and behaviours feel alien. At that point we might convince ourselves that the goals we set were wrong. But this is not necessarily the right conclusion: feeling uncomfortable is only to be expected in the circumstances, and if we persevere the changes are likely to become more stable and 'natural'.

SELF-MONITORING

Some Stoic disciplines could help us to keep things in perspective and maintain a clear awareness of our emotional life. One of these is the practice of spending some time in the morning thinking about the day to come, in order to prepare for what difficulties and challenges might lie ahead. Another is to go over the events of the day at night, asking ourselves whether our reactions had been appropriate:

> [A]s soon as you get up in the morning ask yourself, 'What do I lack in order to be free from passion? What, to enjoy tranquillity? What am I? Am I a mere worthless body? Am I property? Am I reputation?' None of these. What, then? I am a rational creature.
>
> (Epictetus, *The Discourses*, Book 4, Ch. 6, 34)

What, then, is required of you? Go over your actions. '*Where did I trans-gress*: in relation to peace of mind*? What did I do* that was unfriendly, or unsociable, or inconsiderate? *What have I failed to do that I ought to have done* with regard to these matters?'

(Epictetus, *The Discourses*, Book 4, Ch. 6, 35)

These exercises may be altered by revising some of the questions, and instead reflecting on how to act and feel (or whether we acted and felt) appropriately, bearing in mind what in life has real value and what has not. So, for example, we could begin each day by reading through our list of what is important in life, and reminding ourselves of the values we want to live by and the kind of person we want to be. Or we could spend some time in the evening reminding ourselves of the events of the day and the way we acted. How does this relate to the values we want to live by? If there is a discrepancy, what can we do to improve the match? We could also have a 'self-awareness day', during which we keep a diary of all our feelings and moods. We can then review these, asking ourselves whether they are appropriate and in proportion to the situation.

REWARDING OURSELVES FOR OUR SUCCESSES

Rewarding ourselves when we manage to implement the desired changes will reinforce those changes. In this respect Epictetus advised, as a cure for irascibility, to 'offer a sacrifice when you manage to avoid anger thirty days in a row' (Sorabji, 2000, p. 216). Instead of offering a sacrifice we could give ourselves a treat.

A WORD OF CAUTION

We are also instructed to live each day as our last:

Perfection of character: to live your last day, every day, without frenzy, or sloth, or pretense.

(Marcus Aurelius, Book 7, 69)

But perfection should be taken with a pinch of salt. Keeping our emotions in balance requires effort. This effort is worth investing, since it will help us to live a fulfilled, worthwhile and rational life. But perfection is not on the cards. Beyond a certain point, investing in self-improvement is likely to hinder rather than help the quality of our life. Spending *all* one's time and money on the analyst's couch (or in any other therapist's consulting room) could end up being a wild goose chase and stop people getting involved in ultimately more interesting pursuits. According to Nussbaum (2001), the ideal of emotional perfection is not attainable for us; instead, it is crude and tyrannical.

5

Less than Virtue: Developing Self-control

Ideally, if we have developed the virtues, there should be harmony between our judgements and decisions on the one hand and our emotions and desires on the other. In practice, an unfortunate split can arise between judgement and motivation: we come to the considered conclusion that the best course of action for us is A, yet find ourselves inexplicably doing B. This could be due to faulty decision-making and overlooking some factors that should have been given more importance. Equally, however, it may be that although the decision reached *is* the right one, somehow it does not affect our actual motivation.

The experience of acting against our better judgement is a common one. One way of looking at this is that it is our inclinations that matter most and that we should give precedence to 'what feels right' rather than to contrary judgements. But the fact that something feels right is not necessarily a reflection of its *being* right, and may be due only to the presence of a strong habit or strong desire sabotaging our decision. Making changes often involves training ourselves to act in ways that initially 'feel wrong'. From a virtue perspective, if a discrepancy arises between our overall judgement – the judgement we have reached after considering all relevant factors to the best of our ability – and our motivation, the next best thing after virtue is to override our motivation and apply self-control. As we saw in Chapter 3, this is also a first step towards virtue.

These issues often arise in psychotherapy, as people struggle with problems ranging from failing to implement decisions and changing unhelpful habits to a variety of behavioural and substance addictions. In order to assist clients in dealing with these situations we need to help them to clarify the relative value of the different reasons for and against a course of action, and, if the better judgement is upheld, to learn to manage impulses and apply self-control. This is an essential skill to develop in order to live a good life, and by no means requires our turning into unfeeling robots.

That our better judgement, our evaluation of what on balance is best for us in the circumstances, does not always coincide with our immediate motivation, with what we actually feel inclined to do at a particular time, seems undeniable. Two main questions arise in this respect, which form the focus of this chapter:

1. What kinds of mechanisms allow this to happen?
2. What can we do to bring the two into line and implement our better judgement when our motivation is loath to follow?

Ulysses and the Sirens

A paradigmatic case of self-control occurs in the *Odyssey*, when Ulysses is warned by Lady Circe about the dangers posed to the safety of himself and his crew by the Sirens:

> You will come to the Sirens first of all; they bewitch any mortal who approaches them. If a man in ignorance draws too close and catches their music, he will never return to find wife and little children near him and to see their joy at his homecoming; the high clear tones of the Sirens will bewitch him. They sit in a meadow; men's corpses lie heaped up all round them, mouldering upon the bones as the skin decays. You must row past there; you must stop the ears of all your crew with sweet wax that you have kneaded, so that none of the rest may hear the song. But if you yourself are bent on hearing, then give them orders to bind you both hand and foot as you stand upright against the mast-stay, with the rope-ends tied to the mast itself; thus you may hear the two Sirens' voices and be enraptured. If you implore your crew and beg them to release you, then they must bind you fast with more bonds again.
>
> (Homer, *The Odyssey*, pp. 143–4)

He follows the advice, and sails past the Sirens' island safely. Unfortunately most of us are not always so determined and far-sighted, and could do with following Ulysses' example in many daily life situations.

ARISTOTLE ON WEAKNESS OF WILL AND SELF-CONTROL

In early Greek philosophy, it was not considered possible to know the right thing to do and yet want to and/or actually do something different. Socrates held the view that 'no one does wrong willingly', according to which it is impossible to know the good and at the same time pursue evil. Doing something wrong, therefore, must result from ignorance of the good. The problem with this is that it does not seem to fit the fact that human beings sometimes (or even often) do wrong while declaring that they know what the right thing to do is. The mere existence of this phenomenon poses a problem for this or any other theory that considers motivation to follow inescapably from judgement. Plato came to allow that knowledge of the good may be made ineffective by the workings of passion, but this required the agent to be in some way overcome by an 'alien force', entirely disconnected from reason.

Aristotle introduced the term *akrasia*, variously translated as 'weakness of will', 'incontinence' or 'lack of self-control'.[11] Like Plato, Aristotle allowed desire to override reason, but he also introduced some novel distinctions. *Akrasia* involves acting on a desire (in cases where most people would refrain) and contrary to one's true moral judgement, whereas the opposite is true of *enkrateia* (self-control). According to Aristotle, 'the self-controlled person seems to be the same as someone who tends to stand by his calculation, the incontinent the same as someone who tends to depart from it' (*NE*, Book VII, Ch. 1). The person who lacks self-control comes to the correct conclusion about what course of action to follow, but somehow does not bear it in mind when it comes to acting. Aristotle used the examples of being 'asleep, mad or drunk' (*NE*, Book VII, Ch. 3) to illustrate this in-between state of having and not having knowledge of something, or in which our knowledge is 'dormant' for a time. Knowledge could be 'lost' to us as a result of strong emotions or the powerful action of something that physically affects us, which can cloud our judgement and prevent us from acting on the correct conclusion.

Aristotle identified two types of lack of self-control:

1. Impetuosity (when we act to satisfy a desire without thinking).
2. Weakness (when we arrive at the correct conclusion but do not abide by it).

---

[11]While many subtle distinctions are made among these in the context of contemporary philosophy of mind, I use the terms more or less interchangeably. The traditional translation as 'weakness of will' is somewhat misleading, since there is no obvious Greek word for 'will'. I have kept it, however, since it has been extensively used in the contemporary philosophical debate and also has some currency in everyday language.

Weak people deliberate, but because of the way they are affected fail to stand by their decision, while impetuous people are led on by the way they are affected because they have not deliberated.

(*NE*, Book VII, Ch. 7)

But Aristotle also believed that, although the part that wants to act against our better judgement can be quite unreasonable, it is in fact responsive and can be made to listen to reason:

... just as paralysed limbs, when one rationally chooses to move them to the right, are carried off in the opposite direction to the left, so also in the soul: the impulses of incontinent people carry them off in the opposite direction. In the body we do indeed see the lack of control, while in the soul we do not see it; but I think we should nevertheless hold that there is some element in the soul beside reason, opposing and running counter to it. . . . But it does seem to partake in reason, as we said.

(*NE*, Book I, Ch. 13)

ON EATING 'CHOCOLATE NEMESIS'[12]

Let us imagine, using one of Aristotle's own examples, that we have a sweet tooth. This will tend to lead us to eat a slice of chocolate nemesis when given the opportunity, other things being equal. But other things may not be equal: it may be that at the same time we value our health and worry that eating sweet things will damage our teeth, or lead to obesity, diabetes or other physical problems; it may be that we value a slim figure and worry that eating sweet things will lead to our becoming overweight and less attractive. These considerations will tend to lead us to avoid eating the chocolate nemesis should the opportunity arise.

We value things in different ways, some connected with pleasure and short-term gratification, some with long-term benefit, some with more narrowly moral reasons. And sometimes there are conflicts between them. Our valuing the taste of sweet things can clash with our valuing our health and our figures. When a conflict occurs, we need to examine the competing values, rate them in order of importance, reach a considered better judgement as to what we should do in the circumstances and then implement it. It may be that, having weighed up our enjoyment of sweet things, the state of our health and any other relevant

---

[12] A kind of rich chocolate cake.

factors, we conclude that it would be best to refrain from indulging our sweet tooth on the said chocolate nemesis in this particular instance. And it may be that, having arrived at that judgement, we presently proceed to eat the incriminating nemesis.

What has happened is that we have acted on a reason that is relevant (we do value gastronomic enjoyment) but that we ourselves had, all things considered, not judged decisive in that situation (Davidson, 1980; Mele, 1995). Having self-control means acting on what we judge best, overcoming any contrary motivation (refraining from eating the chocolate nemesis even though we feel like eating it, for instance). Acting on a motivating reason that we ourselves had judged less important, on the other hand, shows a lack of self-control. A diagram might show something like this:

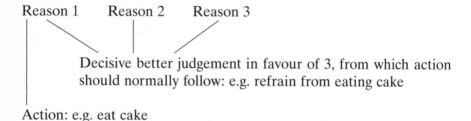

Reason 1   Reason 2   Reason 3

Decisive better judgement in favour of 3, from which action should normally follow: e.g. refrain from eating cake

Action: e.g. eat cake

But why does a partial motivation win out over a considered better judgement that was meant to have taken all relevant factors into account? As has been suggested, one possibility is that the better judgement was wrong in the first place: we just miscalculated the relative value of our reasons (perhaps we were being too rigid in our decision not to eat the cake). But this is by no means universally the case. Aristotle thought that the explanation for this seemingly strange occurrence was that our judgement becomes clouded by some strong desire or physiological factor. In his view the puzzle belonged to the sphere of temperance and self-indulgence (eating, drinking, sex) and was a problem of 'appetite' against reason.

The problem is frequently thought about in these terms, as a situation in which passion and desire overtake reason, or hedonisic choices force themselves upon us at the expense of sensible ones. But it need not be understood in this way. Our better judgement could be said to be 'eudaimonistic', in the sense that it should encompass all factors relevant to the good life, including appetites and emotions (Mele, 1995). And we can act against such a judgement in almost any area of life that we can think of, not just in the 'appetitive' sphere. Nor need it be a matter of emotions versus reason, since there may be powerful emotions both on the side of the better judgement and on the side of the opposing motivation (Mele, 1995).

Davidson (1980) argued that we can act against our better judgement calmly and intentionally, and that the problem should not be reduced to cases of being 'overcome by the beast in us; or failing to heed the call of duty, or of succumbing to temptation' (p. 30). The following is one of the examples that he gives:

> I have just relaxed in bed after a hard day when it occurs to me that I have not brushed my teeth. Concern for my health bids me rise and brush; sensual indulgence suggests I forget my teeth for once. I weigh the alternatives in the light of the reasons: on the one hand, my teeth are strong, and at my age decay is slow. It won't matter much if I don't brush them. On the other hand, if I get up, it will spoil my calm and may result in a bad night's sleep. Everything considered I judge I would do better to stay in bed. Yet my feeling that I ought to brush my teeth is too strong for me: wearily I leave my bed and brush my teeth. My act is clearly intentional, although against my better judgement.

The reward that threatens our better judgement need not even be positive, and could simply be the removal of a negative experience. An alcoholic, for instance, may be motivated to continue to drink partly in order to avoid 'the horrors' (the affectionate name for what is otherwise known as *delirium tremens*). Or we may have arrived at the better judgement that we should stop drinking so much coffee but find it difficult to implement simply because we had underestimated the effort that would be required in changing a long-standing habit.

Action against our better judgement does not occur only in the obvious contexts of changing problematic habits, overcoming carnal temptations or carrying out feats of endurance. It can equally occur in relation to complex daily decisions such as moving to another town, changing jobs or ending a relationship. For instance, we may drop our plans to take up a new challenging job because doing so rids us of uncomfortable feelings of anxiety. When different reasons of similar weight lead us in different directions we may end up questioning an otherwise sound decision and acting against our better judgement. In these cases we need to think through our reasons – including short-term enjoyment, long-term well-being and moral considerations – and weigh up their importance as well as the costs and benefits involved, as was described in Chapter 3.

SHIFTING JUDGEMENT

But we still have to explain how it is possible for motivation at odds with our comprehensive better judgement to end up overriding it. According to Rachlin (2000, p. 3), the problem starts with the fact that, alone in the animal world, human beings are able to experience a conflict between immediate inclination and future considerations: 'A squirrel in its natural environment does not have and does not need self-control.' The problem of self-control is caused by the fact that our evaluations of reward are not stable, but tend to vary depending on how close we are to the reward. When we are at a distance, our evaluation is more objective; when we are closer, our desire increases and it is easier to succumb. Away from the chocolate nemesis we may feel quite clear that, all things considered, eating it would not be best in the circumstances. When it is on a plate in front of us this may dramatically change, and we may find it difficult to resist.

Ainslie (2001, p. 38) also writes about our tendency to 'prefer smaller earlier rewards to larger, later ones temporarily, during the time that they're imminent'.[13] We could ask why this does not count as simply changing our mind. The answer lies in whether an option is chosen even at a distance or only when we are close to it. If on balance the option is not preferred in advance, and is regretted afterwards, this may indicate lack of self-control. As Rachlin (2000) points out, the difficulty with wanting both X now and Y in the future, when these are incompatible, is that the future as such never arrives, and in the present we always prefer X. We want to indulge our sweet tooth and to have a healthy body and slim figure. If these clash, our decisive better judgement may be in favour of the latter. But when we are close to the cake, we prefer it over the longer-term rewards of health and slimness.

Self-control is not strictly about favouring long-term considerations over short-term ones: if you are a workaholic, for instance, it might take a certain amount of self-control to take a day off work; for someone who struggles to turn up at work consistently, on the other hand, effort and application might be required to *avoid* taking time off work. It is only in relation to particular situations and patterns of thought and behaviour that we can decide whether an action should be described as 'self-controlled' or 'giving in to temptation' – where all this need mean is: following a course of action that we do not consider best in the circumstances (Rachlin, 2000). Similarly, if we have arrived at the better

---

[13]This is known as 'hyperbolic discounting'.

judgement that we should give up our job and travel around the world, we will probably need self-control to combat the fear that may well arise as a result of the lack of income and security that we will face.

Mele (1987) writes that action against one's better judgement is both rational and irrational: it is done for reasons, but not the reasons considered best. He suggests a model in which a number of factors contribute to the causation of action in cases of motivational conflict: these can be beliefs, desires and intentions, but also non-rational factors such as how close we are to the source of temptation, how vividly and succulently we imagine it, and our capacity and motivation for self-control. Depending on the balance of these, we will end up acting with or without self-control. Our better judgement is susceptible to shifts that have nothing to do with rational considerations and are due instead to features of the situation like proximity and imagination.

Lack of self-control therefore occurs in cases of motivational split and involves acting on a reason that we ourselves had judged less important than others. Our actions in these cases are influenced by non-rational factors that include habits, appetites and desires, and positive or negative emotions. According to Ainslie (2001) there is continuity between motives in general, hungers and emotions. The line between emotions and other appetites is indistinct, and 'so is the line between appetites and other reasons to seek or avoid things' (p. 66).

BACK TO ARISTOTLE

Aristotle's view was that lack of self-control could happen as a result of either impetuosity (acting without thinking) or weakness (coming to the correct conclusion but not abiding by it because of some strong factors that cloud our understanding and make our judgement ineffective). He used the images of being 'asleep, mad or drunk' as metaphors for the process whereby our judgement becomes clouded. While Aristotle did not spell out his precise views on how we come to act in a way that lacks self-control, what he says could be seen as hinting at a range of cognitive malfunctioning that mediates between the influence of non-rational factors and the akratic action (the action that manifests akrasia).

One mechanism that can lead to lack of self-control is acting impulsively or automatically, without giving ourselves the chance to consider the issues at stake in the present situation. We had reached a better judgement but we act before we are able to link our current action with it. The judgement drops firmly to the back of our mind and disappears from our cognitive horizon (Elster, 2000), which is instead filled by other considerations, influenced by non-rational factors. Or our evaluation of the situation can be distorted by the effect of those factors to the extent that the values we come to attach to different rewards are temporarily at odds with our previous judgement. Either way practical reason is corrupted.

The latter process manifests itself in self-deceived thinking and rationalisations that appear to justify what we are about to do. Self-deceived thinking can be sneaky and difficult to spot, and at the time we often believe our excuses. We need not imagine a hidden inner homunculus scheming to trip us up and sniggering when we fall. As we saw in Chapter 3, self-deception happens unintentionally, through a number of cognitive mechanisms, and boils down to the fact that sometimes our desire to believe something biases the way we go about gathering evidence and/or our evaluation of that evidence.

Going back to the chocolate nemesis in front of us, we may temporarily forget about our previous judgement, as thoughts of the forthcoming pleasure fill our mind. So we may find ourselves eating without even asking ourselves how this fits in with our better judgement. Or we may remember our previous judgement but convince ourselves that one slice will not make any difference, that life would be unbearable without chocolate, that we deserve the treat, that we will begin our diet tomorrow or that we do not really care that much about our weight.

THE ANSWER IS COMMITMENT

If we are under the influence of a strong motivation that threatens our better judgement we need to take steps to prevent ourselves from succumbing to the impulses and shifts in perception that may lead us to act against that judgement. It is important in this respect to have reflected on the issues and come to a sound decision, otherwise we will be more likely to be taken in by self-deceived thinking. What could these steps be?

> The answer is clear: we can do something at the earlier point t_A to prevent ourselves from changing our minds; we can commit ourselves at t_A to the alternative we have chosen, so that at t_B we will either not be able to change our minds or, if we do, the change will be costly.
>
> (Rachlin, 2000, p. 48)

The solution lies in commitment. We need to commit ourselves to the chosen alternative when our motivation is unaffected, and to do something that will stop us changing our mind at a later time, or make the change costly. We should make a 'current choice to restrict the range of future choices' (Rachlin, 2000, p. 50). Since it may not be possible to remove the source of temptation altogether, we need to find other ways to bind ourselves to our better judgement.

Unlike Ulysses, Orpheus did not take such precautionary action. In Greek mythology Orpheus was the son of Apollo and Calliope, and played the lyre enchantingly. His tragic story has been the subject of a number of operas, and there are different versions of it. When his new wife, the nymph Eurydice, dies of a snake's bite, Orpheus is grief-stricken and resolves to go to the underworld to win her back. He makes his way, overcoming obstacles through his music. Pluto, king of the underworld, is moved to pity and agrees that Orpheus may take Eurydice back to earth, on condition that during the journey he does not turn back to look at her even for the briefest glance. They proceed. But in a thoughtless moment, or to check that Eurydice is still follow-ing, Orpheus turns back and loses her for ever. We do not know whether Orpheus had thought of the dangers ahead. But from our vantage point we can see that Orpheus' better judgement should have been not to turn back *under any circumstances*, and that he paid a high price for not taking steps to ensure that this course would be unfailingly pursued.

If, like Ulysses, we want to make sure that we act on our better judgement in the face of contrary motivation, we need to find ways to prevent ourselves from acting otherwise at the time when our judgement is likely to shift. Dennett (2003) describes this as follows: 'Ulysses knows perfectly well the long-term benefits of adopting the policy of avoiding the Sirens when they sing their seductive song, but he also knows he is disposed in many circumstances to overvalue immediate payoffs, so he needs to protect himself from a somewhat misshapen preference structure that he expects will impose itself on him when time t rolls around. . . . His seduction by the Sirens is not *inevitable*, provided he has enough lead time to prepare his avoiding move' (p. 206). Commitment to our better judgement involves think-ing ahead to predict times of vulnerability and taking action to prevent ourselves from acting on future motivation: 'The trick is to arrange it so that "at time t" your will is ineffective' (p. 206). This is not always easy. All sorts of Sirens' songs are liable to get in the way.

Of course acting with or without self-control on one occasion does not in itself make us a self-controlled or weak-willed *person*, since this reflects more of an ongoing *tendency* to give in to inclinations, emotions or desires. For Aristotle, both *akrasia* and *enkrateia* are primarily character traits rather than occasional behaviours. Mele (1987) defines self-control as 'the ability to master motivation that is contrary to one's better judgement' (p. 54) and the self-controlled person as one who is 'disposed to exhibit self-control in appropriate circumstances' (p. 60). He points out, however, that a self-controlled person will not necessarily exhibit self-control at all times and in all areas of life.

THE ELEMENTS OF SELF-CONTROL

On the basis of the above discussion, we could say that the crucial ingredients in developing self-control are:

1. The motivation to be the kind of person who wants to follow a better judgement when motivation is recalcitrant.
2. A sound, thought-through decision. Only if our resolution is strong, if we have no doubts about our better judgement, will we be able to make the necessary effort and withstand the Sirens' song of self-deception.
3. A firm commitment. We should acknowledge that we are in a situation in which we need to guard against our own future motivation, that this is likely to be difficult, and strongly commit ourselves to making the necessary effort.
4. The ability to do this. Perhaps some people manage on the strength of what we could call 'raw willpower'. But for most of us 'willpower' has to mean a willingness to learn and use whatever tricks we can in order to prevent ourselves from acting in ways that are at odds with our better judgement.[14]

Self-control is not an all-or-nothing affair. It comes in degrees, and we should aim to develop it gradually. We must also remember that the

---

[14]Thanks to Peter Worley for making the perceptive point that a view of the will as something we apply *in* situations of temptation (as opposed to a commitment to finding strategies *in advance of* the situation) may itself be used as a form of self-deception. For example, we could tell ourselves that our 'willpower' is all we need to get through a tempting situation when in fact it is clear from past experience that it is not enough, and that we need to make an effort to find specific strategies ahead of the time.

eventual aim is a shift in motivation itself: reaching a point where we do not have to put so much effort into making the change any more, and the relevant feelings and actions just come naturally. Aristotle tells us again and again that repetition and habituation are the key to character change.

> For by acting as we do in our dealings with other men, some of us become just, others unjust; and by acting as we do in the face of danger, and by becoming habituated to feeling fear or confidence, some of us become courageous, others cowardly. The same goes for cases of appetites and anger; by conducting themselves in one way or the other in such circumstances, some become temperate and even-tempered, others intemperate and bad-tempered. In a word, then, like states arise from like activities.
>
> (*NE*, Book II, Ch. 1)

The process of self-transformation might need to start with applying self-control to conquer our wayward motivation. This may seem hopelessly 'wrong' and false at first: especially if a habit or inclination has been with us for a long time, we will have come to see it as just 'the way we are' instead of a form of conditioning that has taken place over time, something we have repeated and rehearsed so often that it appears an inescapable part of us. Doing something different then will feel alien. We need to be vigilant, as we could sneakily use this as an excuse to give up the effort to change: it is just 'not us'. But we should *expect* to feel uncomfortable at first and persevere, since this sense of unfamiliarity can be changed by the diligent practice of a different behaviour. Of course, if an attempt to change evokes feelings of terror, we need to consider the possibility that we have aimed too high, and think of starting with a smaller intermediate change (i.e. aim for the mean between remaining in the comfort zone and straying too far from it).

Self-control can apply both to avoiding doing things that we are motivated to do, as in the cake example, and to pushing ourselves to go through with things that we are in part reluctant to do. The following is an example of the latter.

RUNNING THE LONDON MARATHON

Imagine that you hate running but that despite that you have come to a sound decision to run the London Marathon. Your reasons might be that you value testing yourself, pushing yourself to do things that appear difficult to you, and developing self-discipline and persistence.

These values are really important to you. You are committed to doing this. Is this all you need to implement your decision? Yes and no. Your commitment needs to find expression in concrete ways that will keep you going through those arduous hours of training when, inevitably, the question 'Why am I doing this?' floats to the surface of your mind. If you hate running, this is likely to occur frequently.

At those times you will need to use tricks like: reminding yourself – vividly – of why you *are* doing this, of what there is to be gained and what to be lost by giving up, of the kind of person you want to be; telling people you will be doing this, as a deterrent to giving up; imagining yourself as having achieved your goal, or someone important in your life as being proud of you; rewarding yourself in some way; thinking of some (constructive) penalty for giving up; learning to spot and counteract potentially self-defeating thoughts such as: 'I'll take a break today, I'll start again tomorrow', or 'Perhaps I can do it next year'; and so on.

Along these lines, a sports psychology website (sportsmedicine. upmc.com) offers would-be runners some useful tips for dealing with 'the wall', or the barrier of fatigue that tends to kick in when the body runs out of 'fuel' (i.e. reserves of glycogen) after about 20 miles: 'As your pace slows and running becomes more difficult, your mind has a tendency to worry and focus on negative possibilities. When you begin to panic and the fatigue escalates, soon the word "stop" enters your mind. That's "the wall".' Runners should accept these feelings and keep running (unless of course they are in serious pain, in which case they should stop). The site also advises: 'Instead of thinking about the pain, concentrate on your stride, your breathing, your kick, or other technical aspects of the run. Concentrate on the music in your head, the relief you'll feel after it's over, or the pride you will have when you finish. If you've developed and practiced cue words and inspirational phrases during your training, now is the time to use them.' Another piece of advice is to avoid feeling overwhelmed by breaking the race down into smaller pieces:

> Find runners in the field who you can catch.
> Find spots along the course and run to them.
> Focus on the 'next' mile or the 'next' 30 minutes of running. Surely, you can make it through another mile or another half-hour. String enough of these blocks together and you'll find that you've finished the race.

The difficulty with this kind of situation is that giving up may actually seem fairly reasonable, and in some cases it would be. At what point would we be justified in calling our original decision into question? No doubt there will be many times when we want to. There can be no hard and fast rule about this, although an important piece of the jigsaw is the soundness of that decision. If we feel like revisiting this, it may be due to the following:

1. It was not the right decision in the first place (we thought that testing ourselves to do challenging things was more important than it really was).
2. Something has changed (of course, reconsidering our choice would be the appropriate thing to do if circumstances changed as a result of suffering an injury, for instance).
3. A lack of self-control (we really do value the ability to stand up to this kind of challenge, but we deceive ourselves and are tempted to give up because the relief of discomfort is uppermost in our mind).

In a case like this it may be particularly difficult to be sure whether ideas of retreating are self-deceived thoughts motivated by a desire to avoid discomfort or the voice of reason, telling us that we are pushing ourselves too hard, that something else in our life is suffering and that we should think again. There is no easy answer, although a sound decision and a keen self-awareness should help. As was indicated earlier, a test may consist in how we feel about the decision at a distance. Other cases, however, may be easier to diagnose, such as those involving an 'addiction'.

ADDICTIVE BEHAVIOURS

The preceding discussion has at several points crossed over into the territory of 'addiction', and it may be useful to consider the parallels. The term 'addiction' is a fuzzy one, in some ways best avoided. On the other hand it is a frequently used concept, which many people resort to in order to make sense of their experience, and therefore it seems important to gain some understanding of what being 'addicted' involves.

Nowadays we tend to think of addiction as something that *happens to* (some) people, thereby completely removing their ability to control their behaviour in relation to the relevant substance/activity. This folk usage is a relatively recent one, dating back to the Temperance Movement in the United States. Before the end of the eighteenth century it was thought that people drank because they wanted to rather than because they 'had to'. People who were frequently intoxicated were called drunkards, and if the word 'addicted' was used at all it was in the sense of 'habituated' (to drunkenness) (Levine, 1978). The vocabulary of vice was more commonly employed with regard to drunken behaviour than that of compulsion.

TWO MODELS OF 'ADDICTION'

The late eighteenth and nineteenth centuries saw the development of a new perspective that held as its main points:

(1) the notion of alcohol as an addictive substance;
(2) the drunkard's loss of control over drinking;
(3) the understanding of the condition as a disease; and
(4) abstinence as the only cure.

These, with the significant difference that alcohol was considered addictive only for some congenitally predisposed people, were to become the cornerstones of Alcoholics Anonymous many years later. The AA model was developed after the end of Prohibition in the US in 1933, at a time when alcohol problems were beginning to reappear while at the same time the nation was in no mood for a theory of alcoholism that disallowed moderate consumption. The general AA view is that one is born an alcoholic in virtue of some physiological vulnerability to alcohol. This means that on consuming alcohol alcoholics experience craving (i.e. a compulsion to drink against their will) and lose all power to control intake. The disease is progressive and irreversible and cannot be cured, although it may be arrested by lifelong abstinence. There is a difference between the alcoholic, who is afflicted by a disease, and the excessive drinker, who is not. The differentiating factor between them is the phenomenon of loss of control.

The disease model, which has had several reincarnations since the original formulation, has been criticised on several grounds. The distinction between 'real' alcoholics and mere excessive drinkers is dogmatic and not open to disconfirmation by contrary evidence. And the very application of the notion of disease to goal-directed behaviour has been challenged as incoherent. According to Davies (1992), 'there is a clear difference in the way the word ["symptom"] is being used when (a) we describe something such as high temperature, shortage of breath, or a skin rash, as a symptom, and (b) we talk about going into a pub and buying a pint of beer as a symptom. Whatever we mean by the word "voluntary" . . . it is clear that going into a pub is voluntary in a sense that having a high temperature is not' (p. 48). On the other hand, the development of the disease model was useful in the sense that if people were ill rather than sinners it would become possible to provide services to help them.

The mechanism of craving is often resorted to in order to effect this re-classification of voluntary into non-voluntary behaviour. Davies (1992) points out that 'in ordinary usage, craving is a response to some basic biological need, giving it an implied compulsive quality, and semantically distinguishing it from a simple want. . . . The implication of craving is that the person in question does not simply want, but in some sense has to have, something' (p. 49). He goes on to question what grounds we have for postulating 'an irresistible drive rather than a desire to have' (p. 50).

The main alternative to the disease model is provided by psychological approaches, which aim to explain the processes through which physiological, psychological, social and cultural factors exercise their influence on addictive behaviours. One of the main explanatory concepts is that of *reinforcement*, positive when a behaviour increases as a result of the presence of a pleasant consequence and negative when it increases as a result of the absence of an unpleasant consequence. Drinking, for instance, can be positively reinforced by the feelings of relaxation or sociability induced by alcohol, as well as negatively reinforced by the occurrence of withdrawal symptoms.

Another important concept is that of *self-efficacy*, which refers to a person's evaluation of his or her competence to perform a particular task in a given situation. If self-efficacy is low, the person will have feelings of anxiety and avoid performing the task or attempt it with little effort; the opposite will be the case if self-efficacy is high. Using these two concepts we could say that people drink or use drugs because their use is reinforcing in some way. As use increases, a number of negative consequences begin to accrue, but these are likely to be disregarded in favour of the more immediate rewards. Inner conflict will increase as the balance continues to shift, and self-efficacy will be necessary to implement any behaviour change.

In this model the 'addict' 's psychological mechanisms are no different from anybody else's, and addictive behaviours are governed by the same principles as any other behaviour. Non-substance addictions could then be seen as on a par with substance ones. Orford (1985, p. 319) writes of 'a range of appetitive activities which can become excessive', including eating, sex and gambling. The rewards of these activities can be as powerful and immediate as those of substance use. According to Peele (1985), people become addicted to powerful experiences that modify mood and sensation, whatever their source. The pharmacological action of a substance, however, is likely to create distinctive issues and complications.

LACK OF SELF-CONTROL AND ADDICTION

To what extent do the puzzles of 'addiction' overlap with those of weakness of will and lack of self-control? Self-defeating behaviour has traditionally been difficult to reconcile with rational agency, and has often been explained away as a consequence of the agent's being overwhelmed by some kind of irresistible force that somehow obliterated rational powers. This seemed the only way of solving the philosophical problem of weakness of will so long as the agent was seen as wholly rational. In the disease model, the agent was affected to the point of loss of control by a particular substance. In psychology, on the other hand, subjects were seen as moulded by processes of genetic and environmental conditioning, and the role of volition was overlooked until the reawakening of interest in cognitive processes in the late twentieth century. But recent theorising both in philosophy and in psychology points to a more balanced picture of a rational agent whose actions may be influenced by non-rational factors to varying degrees. In this respect there is some convergence between 'addiction' and weakness of will, both of which could be seen as showing some 'corruption of practical reason' (in Elster, 1999).

For Miller and Brown (1991, p. 9), 'behaviours seem to qualify as *addictive* only when they meet two criteria . . . : [1] they yield immediate gratification, and [2] they involve some degree of diminished volitional control'. In their view, behaviour is affected not only by genetic and environmental factors but also by what they call *self-regulation*, which consists in 'engaging in specific controlling responses in order to alter the probability of one's own subsequent behaviour, usually decreasing or displacing a previously higher-probability behaviour' (p. 7). They suggest that addictive behaviours could be understood in terms of impaired self-regulatory processes.

In normal self-regulation, processes of self-monitoring and self-evaluation – or the ability to recognise internal states and detect discrepancies between our current status and our goals – inform us whether a particular behavioural pattern is working or whether there is a need to make a change. The detection of a discrepancy tends to initiate change, although if the discrepancy is too big, or the person lacks efficacy, an attempt at change may not be made or may be abandoned, in which case defensive cognitive strategies are likely to be adopted in order to reduce the perceived clash ('I can't do it'; 'I didn't want it anyway'). The capacity for self-regulation occurs on a continuum, and some people have more than others: 'genetic, neuropsychological, physiological, and personality characteristics may predispose individuals to experience difficulties in regulating drug use and other behaviours offering short-term gratification' (Miller and Brown, 1991, p. 27). Self-regulation requires a shift from automatic processing, which requires little or no attention, to controlled processing, which is needed when learning new behaviours or modifying old ones.

A similar distinction between automatic and consciously controlled action is offered by Goldman (1994) as a solution to, among other things, the problem of weakness of will. There may be 'two complementary processes that operate in the selection and control of action. The first process is invoked to explain the ability of some action sequences to run off automatically without conscious control or the use of attentional resources, and is used to select simple, well learned, or habitual skills. The second process allows for deliberate conscious control to initiate, guide, or modulate the course of action', and is required for tasks that: '[1] involve planning or decision making, [2] require troubleshooting, [3] are ill-learned or contain novel action sequences, [4] are judged to be dangerous or technically difficult, or [5] require overcoming a strong habitual response or resisting temptation' (Goldman, 1994, pp. 118–19). Goldman suggests that 'so-called akratic actions' may be explained by the fact that the automatic selection mechanism can initiate actions independently of, and even in opposition to, the conscious attentional system.

According to Ainslie (2001, p. 49), 'the defining feature of "addiction" . . . is that the imminent prospect of [activities such as using a substance, overspending, kleptomania, dangerous sex and so on] is strongly rewarding, but they're avoided if foreseen from a distance and regretted afterward'. This, as has been discussed, is just the pattern that all forms of lack of self-control follow. Ainslie considers 'addictions to substances . . . [as] just the most obvious examples of robust, alternating preferences for conflicting goals' (p. 49), while non-substance addictions 'form a conceptual link to a large class of ordinary "bad habits," habits that people say they want to be rid of even while indulging in them' (p. 17).

'Addiction' therefore seems to coincide to a large extent with lack of self-control. In both cases the agent is subject to both rational and non-rational influences. Both involve a motivational split and some process of preference reversal whereby we come to value things differently when we are close to an object of temptation. This 'valuing differently' is seen at a distance as being the result of self-deception and rationalisation. If 'craving', which is often portrayed as the hallmark of addiction, is seen simply as a strong desire, it is clearly one of the mechanisms that can lead to lack of self-control in general.

But 'lack of self-control' seems to have a wider application than 'addiction': it could refer to one-off events, for instance, whereas 'addiction' is normally applied to ongoing patterns. The former may apply to doing or not doing something, whereas the latter tends to refer specifically to doing something (we would not say we are addicted to not exercising). While 'addiction' can be used in relation to the emotions, it is more readily applied to things like habits and appetites. And addictive behaviours tend to be characterised by distinctive processes of tolerance and withdrawal, although this is not universally true and is at any rate much more unclear in relation to the behavioural addictions.

TYING OURSELVES TO THE MAST

While we all start off with varying degrees of capacity for self-control, there is room for self-improvement. If 'temptation' is conceptualised as the inclination to choose the closer reward even though it is the poorer option, then 'willpower' can be the motivation and ability to take steps in advance of the time to counter our own future motivation, and it is this we need to work on in order to develop self-control. It may be that some 'temptations' are near irresistible *at the time*, but we can still take steps towards preparing for them. According to Elster (2000, p. 203): 'The hardest thing is to resist a strong feeling at the moment it arises. . . . An alternative to "instant self-control" is to adopt one of several indirect strategies.'

Two main strategies to resist temptation are: *bunching* and *precommitment* (Elster, 2000). Bunching is a cognitive strategy and consists in casting the choice as not being 'between, say, drinking today and not drinking today, but between drinking today and on all later occasions and not drinking either today or on any later occasion' (p. 187). Precommitment strategies, on the other hand, are behavioural and can take many forms. Elster suggests the following list in relation to substance addiction:

1. putting oneself in a situation where the addictive substance is not available;
2. enlisting other people to protect oneself against oneself;
3. creating a delay between the decision to consume and the time when the substance becomes available;
4. imposing costs on the decision to consume;
5. hypnosis, aversion therapy, and cue-extinction techniques;
6. cue avoidance.

Elster (2000) reports an effective example of (2), 'in a sworn and witnessed statement made by one James Chalmers of New Jersey in 1795: "Whereas, the subscriber, through the pernicious habit of drinking, has greatly hurt himself in purse and person, and rendered himself odious to all his acquaintances and finds that there is no possibility of breaking off from the said practice *but through the impossibility to find liquor*, he therefore begs and prays that no person will sell him for money, or on trust, any sort of spirituous liquor"' (pp. 188–9).

Similarly, Ainslie (2001) writes about four kinds of tactics we can adopt to commit to future choice:

1. Extrapsychic commitment, which involves preventing ourselves from choosing a future option or setting up external incentives that will influence our future choice. 'But devices that tie you to the figurative mast don't act by spoiling your appetite – for drinking or spending money, for instance. They keep you from acting when your appetite is strong.' A lot of the time this method will not require literally tying ourselves to anything, but enlisting other people's help in some way. 'The tactic is to put your reputation in a community at stake' (p. 75).
2. Manipulation of attention, or redirecting the mind away from particular feelings.
3. Preparation of emotion, involving the inhibition of an emotion or the cultivation of a contrary emotion.
4. Personal rules that turn the choice into a matter of principle. But this in itself is not enough, since if there is persistent contrary motivation it is easy to find spurious exceptions to the rule. 'Just this once' is a particularly common one.

In this respect, Ainslie quotes a fitting passage from William James:

How many excuses does the drunkard find when each new temptation comes! It is a new brand of liquor which the interests of intellectual culture in such matters oblige him to test; moreover it is poured out and

it is a sin to waste it; or others are drinking and it would be churlishness
to refuse; or it is but to enable him to sleep, or just to get through this
job of work; or it isn't drinking, it is because he feels so cold; or it is
Christmas day; or it is a means of stimulating him to make a more powerful resolution in favor of abstinence than any he has hitherto made; or it
is just this once, and once doesn't count, etc., etc., *ad libitum* – it is, in
fact, anything you like except being a drunkard.

(Ainslie, 2001, p. 86)

But we must remember that willpower can also have serious side-
effects. Exact rules are easier to enforce than flexible ones, but they
can become too rigid. When the situation is not clear-cut it is difficult
to know whether an exception to a rule is to be considered a lapse or
not, so '[u]nder the influence of an imminent reward you may claim an
exception to a rule, but later think you fooled yourself, that is, see
yourself as having had a lapse' (Ainslie, 2001, p. 147). On the other
hand, it is also possible to be too inflexible in applying a rule 'for fear
that you'll later see your choice as a lapse' (p. 148).

RELAPSE PREVENTION

In the field of addictive behaviours, the kinds of strategies outlined
above are known as 'relapse prevention' (Marlatt and Gordon, 1985).
The idea behind relapse prevention is that implementing a behaviour
change is relatively easy; what is hard is maintaining it (as in the old
Mark Twain quotation: 'Giving up smoking is easy, I've done it hun-
dreds of times'). The cornerstones of relapse prevention are:

1. Self-monitoring to identify high-risk situations, those in which we
   are more likely to succumb to temptation. These could be social,
   emotional or environmental.
2. Developing cognitive, behavioural and environmental strategies to
   deal with high-risk situations and the urges that they might give rise
   to. This includes preparing for a possible lapse so as to minimise its
   severity.
3. Making positive lifestyle changes: addressing lacks and imbalances
   that might make a return to the old behaviour seem attractive.

Behavioural strategies include:

- avoiding a situation altogether;
- giving ourselves treats for successfully dealing with a temptation;

- asking for support;
- getting involved in activities that distract us.

Cognitive strategies include:

- reminding ourselves (vividly) of the positive consequences of change;
- reminding ourselves (vividly) of the negative consequences of no change;
- reminding ourselves that impulses have a limited life-span and will pass;
- investing our attention in something else;
- learning to view mistakes as learning experiences;
- challenging self-deceived thoughts.

We may want to write messages for ourselves, and make sure that we look at them often. If we know that we are likely to encounter a high-risk situation, we need to redouble our efforts and make sure that we have handy a list of techniques that will help us to get through it. We may need to enlist a friend's help. Self-monitoring and planning ahead are central in this enterprise: all these techniques would be pretty useless if we were not aware at the appropriate time that we needed to apply them. A particularly important skill involves identifying and challenging our self-deceived thoughts, or apparent reasons to give in to temptation that would not stand up to scrutiny, as in the passage from William James.

A CASE OF LACK OF SELF-CONTROL

Sean has been involved in a dysfunctional and damaging relationship with Miriam for many years. He has on several occasions decided to finish it, and always, for one reason or another, ended up going back to it, partly as a result of Miriam's pressure. He is aware that the constant stress and turmoil have damaged his health. He is aware that this has absorbed energy that he should have devoted to other things, such as his professional development. Miriam's actions have also led to the end of other budding relationships. All in all, it has been a disaster.

Things get gradually worse, with Miriam acting increasingly irrationally. Finally, after one more infuriating episode, Sean decides to end the relationship once and for all. Miriam continues to pursue Sean, gatecrashing his daily life on a regular basis. His stress and turmoil, and the negative effects on his professional and personal life, continue. But, despite having reached a decisive better judgement to the effect that he should have nothing to do with Miriam ever again, Sean is unable to sever his emotional links with her. Conversations, squabbles and fights continue. After a war of attrition, and suffering from a lapse of self-control, Sean allows the relationship to resume.

Sean has come to the better judgement that the right thing for him to do in this situation is to cut Miriam out of his life completely. But he does not manage to implement it. What has gone wrong? Having come to that better judgement, Sean should have recognised, on the basis of his past experience, that he needed to guard against his own future action or judgement – that he was liable, through impulse or habit or self-deceived and irrational thinking, to get involved in the relationship again. He should therefore, after self-monitoring, have devised an action plan to stick to his decision, and worked jolly hard at implementing it.

Sean would have been helped by avoiding all contact with Miriam, or, if this were not possible, avoiding interacting with her at all costs. This may be difficult to sustain. Old habits die hard, and a crowd of self-deceived thoughts may surface and give an illusion of validity, pushing Sean towards action against his better judgement. Sean should have learned to identify and challenge unhelpful thoughts such as:

- She's not so bad, really.
- She's changed.
- She had a difficult childhood, I should understand.
- I can't bear to see her distressed.
- I can't be provoked like this and not respond.
- I should take care of her.
- She's vulnerable.
- I'll be lonely without her.
- There were some good sides to the relationship.
- We can be friends.

Some of these are just false (the relationship really *was* that bad; Sean *can* learn to bear to see Miriam distressed, or be provoked and not respond; Miriam may *seem* changed, but in the past this has always proved a false impression; Sean does *not* have to take care of her); others may be true (there *may* have been good sides to the relationship; Miriam *may* be vulnerable) but are not decisive reasons for action by

Sean's own lights. In other words, in the overall balance of reasons for and against the relationship, Sean himself had not accorded these particular reasons as much weight as to the reasons against it. The problem is that, on seeing Miriam upset, Sean tends to lose sight of his balance of reasons and his better judgement, while the thought 'I can't bear to upset someone this much' becomes vivid and compelling.

Sean should therefore have *forcefully* reminded himself every day, certainly every time that he thought he was likely to come across Miriam, about the kind of person he wanted to be, the kind of life he wanted to lead and the likely consequences of even a brief interaction with Miriam. He should have reminded himself that, although it is unpleasant to witness distress, let alone think of being the cause of it, he could learn to tolerate it, that change does not have to be comfortable, and that acting on reasons that he himself had identified as not decisive could only be damaging in the long run. He could have reminded himself that impulses pass and that the more we avoid acting on them the easier it is likely to become. He could have practised thought-stopping. He could have asked a friend to support him at times of wavering. He could have made other life-enhancing changes.

A CASE OF SELF-CONTROL

At the age of 50, and with a few near-misses behind him, Ranulph Fiennes was entertaining the idea of giving up polar exploration before his luck ran out and of starting to earn his living doing something safer. He nevertheless decided to embark on one more journey, an unsupported crossing of Antarctica, with all the provisions pulled by himself and his companion. This was apparently ambitious to the point of recklessness. He reports having a number of powerful misgivings, but committed himself to the project anyway.

Although they succeeded in their crossing, this turned out to be the journey from hell. In *Mind over Matter* (1993), the book he has written about the experience, Fiennes describes two fragile human bodies thrown into a hostile environment of intense cold and deep crevasses, carrying too much weight but without enough food or protective gear, enduring frostbite, crotch rot, diverse sores, cuts, wounds and infections, hypoglycaemia and hypothermia, diarrhoea and haemorrhoids, and the loss of one-third of their body weight, not to mention hunger, fear, cold, pain and sheer exhaustion. He does not spare us gruesome details of flesh sticking to clothes and frostbitten penises. It makes for painful reading.

It is clear that the trip was not an enjoyable experience (although it may have been a deeply valuable and meaningful one). The two men suffered great physical hardship, missed their families and were frightened of not returning to them. On several occasions each of them privately regretted the decision to undertake the journey or wished to give it all up. What kept them going?

Some mental devices that Fiennes describes using to cope with the situation were: daydreaming, fantasising about food, stopping himself thinking too far ahead and reminding himself of his family. But these might have proved inadequate, on their own, to deal with such a trying situation. The real conditions for self-control seem to have been 'built into' the experience: there was the public commitment; the commitment to the sponsors; pride; a competitive spirit; and, perhaps most powerfully, there was a potential bill of over $100,000 if they called for evacuation as a result of mere loss of resolve as opposed to a life-and-death situation. This in particular acted as an important 'mast-binding' device.

PRACTICAL APPLICATIONS

Even though clients do not often consult a therapist complaining of a lack of self-control, many daily life difficulties are in fact problems of self-control, and frequently come up in counselling and psychotherapy. Changing habits is one such issue: we may require self-control either to start doing something that we are reluctant to do or to stop doing something that we are motivated to do. Some of these involve appetites that we want to curb (stopping smoking, sticking to a diet, cutting down on drinking), whether or not they deserve the label 'addiction'. Or we have decided to undertake some challenging project but are not wholly enjoying it, and need to find ways to keep ourselves going (running a marathon, doing a PhD). Similarly, we may need self-control to implement resolutions that involve a degree of fear and that we know we will be tempted to abandon (leaving our job to travel around the world, ending a relationship, moving to a different country).

Complex decisions are particularly difficult in this respect. In the case of fear we need to assess whether the fear is due to excessive attachment to the familiar – understandable but not to be acted on – or a sign that the challenge that we have taken on is too big at that particular time. In the case of persevering with a meaningful but burdensome project we have to work out at what point the costs start becoming too high. We should not assume that the answer is obvious. Decisions involving giving up a course of study, hobby or profession, for instance, may be the result either of giving in to short-term considerations, which we are likely later to regret, or of an appropriate realignment of our interests and values. And sometimes self-control is needed for counterintuitive tasks: if we have become used to devoting all our time to a project, it may require a huge effort to go on holiday, as we persuade ourselves that we do not have the time, that we cannot afford it, that the plane might crash and so on.

In all cases of ambivalence we can help clients to understand and assess their values, weigh up competing reasons in decision-making and arrive at a sound resolution. Complex cases, in which it is not clear to clients whether they need metaphorically to tie themselves to the mast or give up the journey and turn back, deserve particular attention. Only when a sound judgement has been reached can self-control strategies and mast-binding devices be explored. Once self-control enters the picture, we can help clients to:

- assess their motivation: if this is low, implementing the decision will require constant vigilance;
- assess their confidence: if this is low, they will need to find ways to increase it;
- decide how they can commit themselves to the resolution;
- monitor the relevant behaviour and/or the urges to perform it;
- discover their high-risk situations (places, times, people, moods, activities), since these are the times of highest 'temptation', which will require most effort;
- find practical strategies to deal with these. These may include:
  - thinking about the negative consequences of not changing;
  - thinking about the positive consequences of changing;
  - identifying situations to avoid;
  - identifying situations to encourage;
  - finding activities that instigate a positive frame of mind;
  - locating sources of support that they can call on;
  - recognising and challenging self-deceived thoughts;
  - separating valid reasons from rationalisations.

It is particularly important to examine and challenge any form of self-deception that might make invalid reasons appear valid: if, for instance, our experience tells us that we have tried countless times to control our drinking and failed, and if we know that the consequences of returning to drinking are likely to be dire, then there will be no good reason to drink, ever, and *any* reasons in favour of drinking will be self-deceived ones.

The 'emergency pack' is a useful tool in relapse prevention. The idea is that at times of temptation, when it is easiest to lose perspective and return to our old ways, we can refer to something concrete that will help us to regain the vision we are in danger of abandoning. This might contain: statements about what we have to lose and what to gain by acting on an impulse; reminders about activities that we have found useful in getting over similar moments before; telephone numbers of people who are willing and able to support us; inspiring readings, images or simply helpful perspectives; photographs (for example, of loved ones, or of ourselves at particularly good or bad times); and anything else that might contribute to jolt us out of a negative state and into a more positive one. While this method belongs to a set of strategies designed to counter addictive behaviours, something similar could equally well be employed in any situation characterised by ambivalence and in which self-control is an issue.

Finally, we must remember that self-control is an intrinsic part of training our emotions on the road to virtue, and so we do not need 'a problem' to start making an effort to change. If clients have reflected on themselves and their lives and have come to the conclusion that they want to become more generous, less prone to anger or more courageous, all the methods outlined above may be used in the service of that goal.

6

Conclusion: In Defence of Reason

I have suggested that we have much to gain by tapping into ancient Greek notions of virtue and the good life. If updated and adapted for a modern context, those understandings can provide us with a framework to reflect on what is valuable in life, learn to make good decisions, develop the virtues of character and apply self-control when necessary. While the ideas that I have presented are in some ways close to common sense, they are also somewhat 'subversive' in an era characterised by deep suspicions about reason. A defence of reason would clearly deserve a whole book, probably consisting of several volumes. In what follows I will offer only a few reflections on the subject.

'KNOW THYSELF'

According to Cottingham (1998, p. 27), the most daunting obstacle to the 'philosophical goal of striving for a life guided by a rationally informed vision of the good' is 'a radical loss of confidence in the power of human reason itself', which he traces primarily to 'the steady advance of psychoanalytic modes of understanding' (p. 27). It cannot be denied that we live in a Freudian era, one in which psychoanalytic language and concepts permeate our daily life. We have become used to seeking unconscious, childhood-related motives for our feelings and actions, so that remaining at the conscious level has come to be seen as a sort of evasion, an unwillingness to deal with the 'real' issues. Sometimes the popularity of that kind of explanation appears to be taken as evidence of its truth, but of course the diffusion of psychoanalytic concepts is no indication of their soundness.

For Cottingham (1998), psychoanalytic insights undermine the whole philosophical enterprise of searching for the good life in so far as this involves ideas of self-transparency and self-awareness. He points out that psychoanalysis has shown us that we are opaque to ourselves and often grossly ignorant of our reasons for doing things. Our beliefs and desires are vulnerable to systematic distortions due to past influences. He writes that these distortions may be inaccessible to any enquiry other than a fully 'therapeutic' one, in which we 'lift the veil on the inner structure of our irrational desires and passions, and begin the process of coming to terms with their deeper significance for our emotional equilibrium' (p. 52). Through 'a prolonged and painful struggle [we may] rediscover and reinterpret the dark roots [of] our emotional lives, buried in the half-forgotten patterns of response laid down in early childhood' (p. 59). He also writes that the reintegration of our unconscious does not happen through introspection but through 'a long process of recovery, rehabilitating those parts of the self which are initially submerged beneath the level of ordinary everyday awareness' (p. 140).

Elsewhere, however, Cottingham (1998, p. 132) claims that there is a 'sense in which psychoanalytic theory simply carries the . . . [Socratic self-examination] forward, albeit in a more radically introspective fashion'. The question is what sort of process this 'lifting the veil' on our inner life needs to be. What does 'Know thyself' really mean? There are different and competing views about what 'unconscious' means and how we go about reintegrating it. Cottingham himself writes that 'there can be mental activity which falls short of full reflective awareness', 'confused and fleeting mental activity of a kind which often does not, as it were, reach the transparent surface of consciousness because the relevant kind of attention is absent, or the attention is directed elsewhere' (p. 12). Through this formulation Cottingham arrives at a notion of reintegrating the unconscious that is not peculiarly Freudian: 'after acknowledging its lack of total mastery, our conscious power of understanding can eventually get to grips with those buried images, drives and fears that at first seemed to deny us mastery in our own house. The results of psychoanalysis drag into the light truths which, once we see them, we can recognize that, in a sense, we knew all along' (p. 131).

There are two ways of understanding the process of assimilating material that is not fully integrated in consciousness: as a search for reasons or a search for causes.[15] Cioffi[16] explains that, according to

---

[15]The philosophy of mind debate about whether reasons can be causes is not addressed here.
[16]Notes from a lecture given on 17/12/1989.

Wittgenstein, to give the cause of a state of mind is to put forward an explanatory hypothesis about it, and the appropriate method to determine whether this is true or not is by empirical investigation. To give a reason, on the other hand, involves giving a further description of it, an elaboration of its implicit content. Here the appropriate method is reflection, and the description is acceptable only if the person in question endorses it. An explanation is external to a state of mind, whereas a further elaboration is logically connected with it. States of mind have a history, but they also acquire a particular character by virtue of their relationship to other images and events. The role of psychotherapeutic conversation is to bring more of these connections into consciousness.

The question 'Why do I drink?', for instance, could be answered either in relation to possible *causal* explanations (genetic factors, childhood experiences and so on) or to a person's *reasons* to drink (e.g. it is enjoyable, it is a social lubricant, it lifts the mood). While the former may constitute interesting information, it is the latter that are more fruitfully open to exploration and modification (of course the two are not mutually exclusive, and we can usefully reflect on the historical development of certain emotions, values or beliefs). The hunt for the Freudian unconscious is traditionally conceived of as a search for causes. It is true that 'The psychoanalytic process aims to achieve a radically new perspective on our inmost desires and drives – one which, quite literally, reinterprets our past and present actions and choices' (Cottingham, 1998, p. 144). But this interpretation is distinct from anything that we could achieve through reflection, and its validity could be questioned. It is at any rate utterly discontinuous with a self-examination of the Socratic kind.

There are other ways of conceptualising therapeutic work that operate more on the level of reasons. Lahav (1995), in relation to philosophical counselling, uses as an analogy the distinction between on the one hand analysing a work of art in terms of its own features, and on the other hand trying to unearth the events in the psychology of the artist that might have led to the creation. Along similar lines, and writing about existential counselling, van Deurzen (2002) writes that the process of shedding light on the client's particular way of being involves 'making the implicit explicit' (p. 29).

It is not the case that we have to choose between believing in perfect self-awareness or in the dictates of psychoanalysis. It would be foolish nowadays to try to uphold full and absolute self-awareness and self-control. Dennett (2003, p. 246) writes that 'Consciousness of the springs of action is the exception, not the rule'. He also writes about the need to 'fend off the absolutism that sees only two possibilities: Either we are perfectly rational or we are not rational at all' (p. 271). It is an increasingly accepted fact that we are imperfectly rational animals, vulnerable to all sorts of cognitive biases and blind spots, some of which have already been described. Myers (2004, p. 4) writes about the extent to which 'thinking occurs not on stage, but off stage, out of sight'. But it is nevertheless possible to 'fortify our rationality, to sharpen our thinking, to deepen our wisdom' (p. 247). We can accept that 'important parts of the self are not fully transparent to the deliberations of reason' (Cottingham, 1998, p. 6) without having to deny all rationality and without being forced to jump on the psychoanalytic train.

Nussbaum (2001) acknowledges that adult emotions are shaped by their history, and that the past may have a distorting influence on the present in this respect. She writes that in order to attain greater awareness of our present responses it is important to understand what she calls the 'narrative structure' of an emotion. She also warns that the ideal of emotional perfection is unattainable and tyrannical. We could say that, although our mind is not and never will be fully transparent, it is possible to gain more insight into it by investigating how we came to acquire certain beliefs and how they fit in with other beliefs, by exposing unarticulated theories, hidden assumptions, faulty implications and value conflicts, and generally by examining the patterns and structures of our mental landscape.[16] This process involves reason and reflection.

RATIONAL ANIMALS

Other attacks on rationality are more global. In *Straw Dogs* Gray states, vividly, that 'For Gaia,[17] human life has no more meaning than the life of slime mould' (2002, p. 33). He portrays human beings as a prolific, rapacious, powerful but fundamentally irrational species with overinflated views of its own importance and insight, likely to be destroyed by its own success in the shape of sheer numbers or the backfiring of technology. We are wrong in viewing ourselves as persons who make choices through which we exercise conscious control over

---

[16]Lahav (1995) calls this process 'worldview interpretation'.
[17]'Gaia' is the name that James Lovelock uses for his theory of the Earth as a self-regulating organism, referring to the ancient Greek goddess of the Earth (in Gray, 2002).

our lives. In fact we are not the authors of our actions but the products of necessity, and cannot be responsible for what we do. In sum, we are unimportant, irrational and not even unified selves, let alone responsible ones. There is much that we can readily agree with here: we cannot leave our animal nature behind, our rationality and knowledge of the world are likely to be severely limited, and if we look at ourselves 'from the outside' we can see that our lives are not very significant from the point of view of the universe. But the case can be overstated.

According to Nagel (2000), the feeling we sometimes have that life is absurd arises from our ability to see ourselves through two conflicting perspectives. 'Leading a human life is a full time occupation, to which everyone devotes decades of intense concern' (p. 179): we make choices and plans, we devote energy and attention to our activities, allocating to them varying degrees of importance. 'Yet humans have the special capacity to step back and survey themselves, and the lives to which they are committed, with that detached amazement which comes from watching an ant struggle up a heap of sand' (p. 179). But this recognition of contingency and arbitrariness coexists with a deep engagement with life that for most of us seems entirely non-negotiable: just because as a species we may be irrelevant in the greater scheme of things, it does not follow that individual lives have to be meaningless.

It may well be the case that there is no such thing as a discrete self[18] and that free will turns out to be something much more circumscribed than had previously been wished for. But what follows from this? It does not seem feasible for us to go through life feeling like irrelevant creatures made up of unintegrated parts and with no say in how our lives develop. Acting that way would be a sure route to a psychiatric diagnosis. And believing that there are 'selves' who make choices does not involve commitment to metaphysical views about immaterial souls with absolute freedom. We are meaning-making animals who perceive themselves as unified and as making decisions about all sorts of things. This is what a human life is crucially about. It seems more promising to tone down than to give up our claims to autonomy and rationality.

Dennett (2003) writes that human agents developed from very humble origins: 'at the beginning of life there was no freedom, no intelligence, no choice, but only proto-freedom, proto-choice, proto-intelligence' (p. 143). As organisms became more complex, they developed to the point where there were brains like ours that were designed

---

[18]Dennett (1984) writes about the self as a 'locus of self-control' (p. 81).

by evolution to gather and evaluate information and use it to plan for the future. This process was aided by the development of language and culture. But although our freedom is much greater than that of jellyfish and birds, it has evolved from 'more modest components and predecessors' (p. 143). 'Free will is like the air we breathe, . . . but it is not only not eternal, it evolved, and is still evolving. . . . The atmosphere of free will is . . . the enveloping, enabling, life-shaping, conceptual atmosphere of intentional action, planning and hoping and promising – and blaming, resenting, punishing, and honoring. We all grow up in this *conceptual* atmosphere, and we learn to conduct our lives in the terms it provides' (p. 10).

We should certainly be humble about our importance, the limits of reason, and how much of the world and ourselves we can really understand. We should be a little sceptical about grand theories of human nature. But we should avoid setting up straw men of perfect rationality and pure unsullied self-awareness. It is not an 'either–or': we can accept our inescapable limitations without denying that there is such a thing as rationality or that it has any value, that we can be persons who are responsible and make choices, that our lives can be more or less flourishing and that we have some capacity to move towards the former. Neither viewing ourselves as slime mould nor as demi-gods does us justice, and in the end Aristotle's suggestion that we are rational animals may still best capture our condition in life. Everything else flows from this.

References

Ainslie, G. (2001) *Breakdown of Will*. New York: Cambridge University Press.

Annas, J. (1993) *The Morality of Happiness*. New York: Oxford University Press.

Anscombe, G. E. M. (1958) Modern moral philosophy. *Philosophy*, 33, 1–19.

Aristotle (2000) *Nicomachean Ethics* (trans. R. Crisp). Cambridge: Cambridge University Press.

Aristotle (2002) *Nicomachean Ethics* (trans. S. Broadie/C. Rowe). Oxford: Oxford University Press.

Baggini, J. (2002a) *Philosophy: Key Texts*. Basingstoke: Palgrave.

Baggini, J. (2002b) *Making Sense*. Oxford: Oxford University Press.

Baggini, J. (2004) *What's It All About? Philosophy and the Meaning of Life*. London: Granta.

Bandler, R. & Grinder, J. (1982) *Reframing*. Moab, UT: Real People Press.

Batchelor, S. (1998) *Buddhism Without Beliefs*. London: Bloomsbury (New York: Riverhead, 1997).

Ben Ze'ev, A. (2000) *The Subtlety of Emotions*. Cambridge, MA: MIT Press.

Blackburn, S. (1998) *Ruling Passions*. Oxford: Clarendon Press.

Blackburn, S. (2001) *Being Good*. Oxford: Oxford University Press.

de Botton, A. (2000) *The Consolations of Philosophy*. London: Hamish Hamilton.

Broadie, S. (1991) *Ethics with Aristotle*. New York: Oxford University Press.

Calhoun, C. (2003) Cognitive emotions?, in: R. Solomon (ed.), *What is an Emotion? Classic and Contemporary Readings* (2nd edition). New York: Oxford University Press.

Camus, A. (1975) *The Myth of Sisyphus*. London: Penguin.

Cannon, W. B. (2003), extract from Bodily changes in pain, hunger, fear and rage, in: R. Solomon (ed.), *What is an Emotion? Classic and Contemporary Readings* (2nd edition). New York: Oxford University Press.

Cohen, E. D. & Cohen, G. S. (1999) *The Virtuous Therapist: Ethical Practice of Counseling and Psychotherapy.* Belmont, CA: Wadsworth.

Cooper, M. (2003) *Existential Therapies.* London: Sage.

Cottingham, J. (1998) *Philosophy and the Good Life.* Cambridge: Cambridge University Press.

Crisp, R. (1996) *How Should One Live?* Oxford: Clarendon Press.

Crumbaugh, J. (1973) *Everything to Gain.* Berkeley, CA: Institute of Logotherapy Press.

Csikszentmihalyi, M. (1992) *Flow: The Psychology of Happiness.* London: Rider.

Csikszentmihalyi, M. (1997) *Living Well.* London: Weidenfeld & Nicolson.

Cullity, G. & Gaut, B. (eds) (1997) *Ethics and Practical Reason.* New York: Oxford University Press.

Damasio, A. (1994) *Descartes' Error. Emotion, Reason and the Human Brain.* New York: Putnam.

Darwall, S. (ed.) (2003) *Virtue Ethics.* Oxford: Blackwell.

Davidson, D. (1980) How is weakness of will possible?, in: D. Davidson, *Essays on Actions and Events.* Oxford: Clarendon Press.

Davies, J. B. (1992) *The Myth of Addiction.* Reading: Harwood.

Dawkins, R. (1995) *River out of Eden.* London: Weidenfeld & Nicolson.

De Sousa, R. (2003) extract from The rationality of emotions, in: R. Solomon (ed.), *What is an Emotion? Classic and Contemporary Readings* (2nd edition). New York: Oxford University Press.

Dennett, D. C. (1984) *Elbow Room.* Cambridge, MA: MIT Press.

Dennett, D. C. (2003) *Freedom Evolves.* New York: Allen Lane.

van Deurzen, E. (2002) *Existential Counselling and Psychotherapy in Practice.* London: Sage.

Dyer, G. (1997) *Out of Sheer Rage.* London: Abacus.

Ekman, P. (2003) extract from Biological and cultural contributions to body and facial movement in the expression of emotions, in: R. Solomon (ed.), *What is an Emotion? Classic and Contemporary Readings* (2nd edition). New York: Oxford University Press.

Elster, J. (1999) *Alchemies of the Mind.* New York: Cambridge University Press.

Elster, J. (2000) *Strong Feelings.* Cambridge, MA: MIT Press.

Epictetus (1983) *The Handbook* (trans. N. P. White). Indianapolis, IN: Hackett.

Epictetus (1995) *The Discourses* (trans. Gill/Hard). London: Dent.

Fiennes, R. (1993) *Mind Over Matter.* London: Mandarin.

Foot, P. (1978) *Virtues and Vices.* Oxford: Blackwell.

Foot, P. (2001) *Natural Goodness.* Oxford: Clarendon Press.

Frankl, V. (1959) *Man's Search for Meaning.* London: Rider.

Frijda, N. (2003) Emotions are functional, most of the time, in: R. Solomon (ed.), *What is an Emotion? Classic and Contemporary Readings* (2nd edition). New York: Oxford University Press.

Furedi, F. (2003) *Therapy Culture: Cultivating Vulnerability in an Uncertain Age.* London: Routledge.

Goldman, A. I. (1994) Action (2), in: S. Guttenplan (ed.), *A Companion to the Philosophy of Mind.* Oxford: Blackwell.

Gray, J. (2002) *Straw Dogs: Thoughts on Humans and Other Animals.* London: Granta.

Grayling, A. C. (2003) *What is Good?* London: Weidenfeld & Nicolson.

Greenberger, D. & Padesky, C. A. (1995) *Mind Over Mood.* New York: Guilford Press.

Griffin, J. (1986) *Well-being.* New York: Clarendon Press.

Griffiths, P. (2003) extract from What emotions really are, in: R. Solomon (ed.), *What is an Emotion? Classic and Contemporary Readings* (2nd edition). New York: Oxford University Press.

Guignon, C. (ed.) (1999) *The Good Life.* Indianapolis, IN: Hackett.

Hadot, P. (1995) *Philosophy as a Way of Life.* Oxford: Blackwell.

Homer (1980) *The Odyssey* (trans. W. Shewring). Oxford: Oxford University Press.

Honderich, T. (ed.) (1995) *The Oxford Companion to Philosophy.* Oxford: Oxford University Press.

Hughes, G. J. (2001) *Aristotle on Ethics.* London: Routledge.

Hurka, T. (1993) *Perfectionism.* New York: Oxford University Press.

Hursthouse, R. (1999) *On Virtue Ethics.* Oxford: Oxford University Press.

James, W. (2003) extract from What is an emotion?, in: R. Solomon (ed.), *What is an Emotion? Classic and Contemporary Readings* (2nd edition). New York: Oxford University Press.

Jeffers, S. (1978) *Feel the Fear and Do It Anyway.* London: Arrow Books.

Jopling, D. A. (1996) Philosophical counselling, truth and self-interpretation. *Journal of Applied Philosophy*, 13, 3.

Kekes, J. (1988) *The Examined Life.* Philadelphia P. A.: Pennsylvania State University Press.

Kekes, J. (1995) *Moral Wisdom and Good Lives.* Ithaca, NY: Cornell University Press.

Klemke, E. D. (ed.) (2000) *The Meaning of Life.* New York: Oxford University Press.

Kundera, M. (1985) *The Unbearable Lightness of Being.* London: Faber and Faber.

Lahav, R. (1995) A conceptual framework for philosophical counseling: worldview interpretation, in: R. Lahav & M. da Venza Tillmanns (eds), *Essays on Philosophical Counseling.* Lanham, MD: University Press of America.

Langmuir, E. (1993) *Mountaincraft and Leadership.* The Scottish Sports Council and the Mountainwalking Leader Training Board.

Larmore, C. (1999) The idea of a life plan, in: E. F. Paul, F. D. Miller & J. Paul (eds), *Human Flourishing.* New York: Cambridge University Press.

Lazarus, R. (2003) extract from Appraisal: the minimal cognitive prerequisites of emotion, in: R. Solomon (ed.), *What is an Emotion? Classic and Contemporary Readings* (2nd edition). New York: Oxford University Press.

LeBon, T. (2001) *Wise Therapy.* London: Continuum.

LeDoux, J. (1998) *The Emotional Brain: The Mysterious Underpinnings of Emotional Life.* New York: Touchstone.

Levine, H. (1978) The discovery of addiction: changing conceptions of habitual drunkenness in America. *Journal of Studies on Alcohol,* 39, 143–76.

McDowell, J. (1995) Eudaimonism and realism in Aristotle's *Ethics,* in: R. Heinaman (ed.), *Aristotle and Moral Realism.* London: UCL Press.

McDowell, J. (2003) Virtue and reason, in: S. Darwall (ed.), *Virtue Ethics.* Oxford: Blackwell.

MacIntyre, A. (1985) *After Virtue.* London: Duckworth.

Marar, Z. (2003) *The Happiness Paradox.* London: Reaktion Books.

Marcus Aurelius (2003) *Meditations* (trans. G. Hays). London: Weidenfeld & Nicolson.

Marlatt, G. A. & Gordon, J. R. (1985) *Relapse Prevention.* New York: The Guilford Press.

Mele, A. R. (1987) *Irrationality: An Essay on Akrasia, Self-Deception, and Self-Control.* New York: Oxford University Press.

Mele, A. R. (1995) *Autonomous Agents: From Self-Control to Autonomy.* New York: Oxford University Press.

Mele, A. R. (2001) *Self-Deception Unmasked.* Princeton, NJ: Princeton University Press.

Miller, W. R. & Brown, J. M. (1991) Self-regulation as a conceptual basis for the prevention and treatment of addictive behaviours, in: N. Heather, W. R. Miller & J. Greeley (eds), *Self-control and the Addictive Behaviours.* Botany: Maxwell Macmillan Publishing Australia.

Millgram, E. (ed.) (2001) *Varieties of Practical Reasoning.* Cambridge, MA: MIT Press.

de Montaigne, M. (1958) *Essays* (trans. J. M. Cohen). London: Penguin.

Myers, D. G. (2004) *Intuition: Its Powers and Perils.* New Haven, CT: Yale University Press.

Nagel, T. (1980) Aristotle on eudaimonia, in: A. O. Rorty (ed.), *Essays on Aristotle's Ethics.* Berkeley, CA: University of California Press.

Nagel, T. (2000) The absurd, in: E. D. Klemke (ed.), *The Meaning of Life.* New York: Oxford University Press.

Norem, J. (2002) *The Positive Power of Negative Thinking.* New York: Basic Books.

Nozick, R. (1989) *The Examined Life.* New York: Simon & Schuster.

Nussbaum, M. C. (1993) Non-relative virtues: an Aristotelian approach, in: M. Nussbaum & A. Sen (eds), *The Quality of Life*. Oxford: Clarendon Press.

Nussbaum, M. C. (1994) *The Therapy of Desire*. Princeton, NJ: Princeton University Press.

Nussbaum, M. C. (1995) Aristotle on human nature and the foundation of ethics, in: J. E. J. Altham & R. Harrison (eds), *World, Mind, and Ethics*. Cambridge: Cambridge University Press.

Nussbaum, M. C. (2001) *Upheavals of Thought*. New York: Cambridge University Press.

Nussbaum, M. C. (2003) Emotions as judgements of value and importance, in: R. Solomon (ed.), *What is an Emotion? Classic and Contemporary Readings* (2nd edition). New York: Oxford University Press.

Orford, J. (1985) *Excessive Appetites: A Psychological View of Addictions*. Chichester: Wiley.

Paul, E. F., Miller, F. D. & Paul, J. (eds) (1999) *Human Flourishing*. New York: Cambridge University Press.

Pearsall, P. (2002) *Toxic Success: How to Stop Striving and Start Thriving*. Makawao, HI: Inner Ocean Publishing.

Peele, S. (1985) *The Meaning of Addiction*. Lexington, MA: D. C. Heath.

Peterson, C. & Seligman, M. E. P. (2004) *Character Strengths and Virtues: A Handbook and Classification*. New York: Oxford University Press.

Quennell, P. (1988) *The Pursuit of Happiness*. Oxford: Oxford University Press.

Rachlin, H. (2000) *The Science of Self-Control*. Cambridge, MA: Harvard University Press.

Radcliffe Richards, J. (2000) *Human Nature after Darwin: A Philosophical Introduction*. London: Routledge.

Rasmussen, D. B. (1999) Human flourishing and the appeal to human nature, in: E. F. Paul, F. D. Miller & J. Paul (eds), *Human Flourishing*. New York: Cambridge University Press.

Raz, J. (1999) *Engaging Reason: On the Theory of Value and Action*. New York: Oxford University Press.

Rhinehart, L. (1999) *The Dice Man*. London: HarperCollins.

Rorty, A. O. (ed.) (1980) *Essays on Aristotle's Ethics*. Berkeley, CA: University of California Press.

Russell, B. (1975) *The Conquest of Happiness*. London: Routledge.

Sartre, J.-P. (1958) *Being and Nothingness: An Essay on Phenomenological Ontology*. London: Routledge.

Seeburger, F. F. (1997) *Emotional Literacy*. New York: Crossroad.

Seligman, M. E. P. (2003) *Authentic Happiness*. London: Nicholas Brealey.

Seneca (2003) extract from *De Ira*, in: R. Solomon (ed.), *What is an Emotion? Classic and Contemporary Readings* (2nd edition). New York: Oxford University Press.

Schachter, S. & Singer, J. E. (2003) Cognitive, social, and physiological deter-
minants of emotional state, in: R. Solomon (ed.), *What is an Emotion?*
Classic and Contemporary Readings (2nd edition). New York: Oxford
University Press.

Shigematsu, S. (1988) *A Zen Harvest: Japanese Folk Zen Sayings.* San
Francisco, CA: North Point Press.

Solomon, R. (1993) *The Passions: Emotions and the Meaning of Life.*
Indianapolis, IN: Hackett.

Solomon, R. (1999) *The Joy of Philosophy: Thinking Thin versus the*
Passionate Life. New York: Oxford University Press.

Solomon, R. (ed.) (2003) *What is an Emotion? Classic and Contemporary*
Readings (2nd edition). New York: Oxford University Press.

Sorabji, R. (2000) *Emotions and Peace of Mind.* Oxford: Oxford University
Press.

Statman, D. (ed.) (1997) *Virtue Ethics.* Edinburgh: Edinburgh University
Press.

Storr, A. (1989) *Solitude.* London: Flamingo.

Sutherland, S. (1992) *Irrationality.* London: Penguin.

Taylor, C. (1991) *The Ethics of Authenticity.* Cambridge, MA: Harvard
University Press.

Thagard, P. (2001) How to make decisions: coherence, emotion and practical
inference, in E. Millgram (ed.), *Varieties of Practical Reasoning.* Cambridge,
MA: MIT Press.

Thoreau, H. D. (1983) *Walden* and *Civil Disobedience.* New York: Penguin.

Urmson, J. O. (1980) Aristotle's doctrine of the mean, in: A. O. Rorty (ed.),
Essays on Aristotle's Ethics. Berkeley, CA: University of California
Press.

Warburton, N. (1996) *Thinking from A to Z.* London: Routledge.

Watson, G. (1977) Scepticism about weakness of will. *Philosophical Review,*
86, 316–39.

Watson, G. (1997) On the primacy of character, in: D. Statman (ed.), *Virtue*
Ethics. Edinburgh: Edinburgh University Press.

Wiggins, D. (1980) Deliberation and practical reason, in: A. O. Rorty (ed.),
Essays on Aristotle's Ethics. Berkeley, CA: University of California
Press.

Williams, B. (1985) *Ethics and the Limits of Philosophy.* London: Fontana.

Yalom, I. (1980) *Existential Psychotherapy.* New York: Basic Books.

Index